THE COMPLETE GUIDE TO

FLOORS, WALLS, AND CEILINGS

A Comprehensive Do-it-Yourself Handbook

GARY D. BRANSON

BETTERWAY PUBLICATIONS, INC.
WHITE HALL, VIRGINIA

Published by Betterway Publications, Inc.
P.O. Box 219
Crozet, VA 22932
(804) 823-5661

Cover photo courtesy of Armstrong World Industries
Prepress Services by Studio 500 Associates

Copyright © 1992 by Gary D. Branson

Library of Congress Cataloging-in-Publication Data
Branson, Gary D.
   The complete guide to floors, walls, and ceilings:
a comprehensive do-it-yourself handbook / Gary D. Branson.
      p. cm.
   Includes index.
   ISBN 1-55870-230-X : $14.95
   1. Interior walls—Amateurs' manuals. 2. Floors—Amateurs' manuals.
   3. Ceilings—Amateurs' manuals. I. Title.
TH2239.B73 1992
643'.7—dc20   91-43119
                                                                    CIP

Printed in the United States of America
0 9 8 7 6 5 4 3 2

THE COMPLETE GUIDE TO

FLOORS, WALLS, AND CEILINGS

Other books by Gary D. Branson

The Complete Guide to Barrier-Free Housing
The Complete Guide to Lumber Yards and Home Centers
The Complete Guide to Recycling at Home
The Complete Guide to Remodeling Your Basement

For my children: Cathy, Stephen, James, and David.

Acknowledgments

Thanks go to the following for supplying photographs, illustrations, and/or materials for this book.

Gold Bond Manufacturing Inc.

InFloor Heating Systems

Plywood Paneling Council

Sears

Stanley Tools

United States Gypsum

Wal-Board Tools

Contents

Introduction

Writing a book on the home interior — floors, walls, and ceilings — is for me a sort of homecoming. During the post-World War II years, at the beginning of a national housing boom, my father had gone into business as a drywall (wallboard) contractor. He gave me a job and taught me wallboard work in the summer of my thirteenth year. At the age of nineteen I joined the plasterers' union in order to work on a school building in Wichita, Kansas; at age twenty-two I joined the painters' union to work on a housing project in Minneapolis, Minnesota. As the years passed I became involved in a variety of remodeling projects and tried almost every type of construction work, but the house interior provided my "basic training." The information found in these pages on the subjects of plaster, wallboard, and painting is the result of my own personal hands-on experience gained by wielding the trowel and plasterer's hawk, the lathing hatchet and the paint brush.

Some of the observations given about flooring are from my own experience in building and remodeling. Much of the information regarding carpeting and vinyl floor covering I got by interviewing my son James Branson, who has worked as a floor covering contractor and installer for the past twelve years.

Some fifteen years ago I gave up the construction business and began writing in the construction field. I was for ten years the technical/senior editor for *The Family Handyman* magazine, and helped put together a half-dozen books as well. I am now contributing editor for *Workbench* magazine, and my work is also seen in *Popular Mechanics*. I have done talk radio on a nationwide basis and have appeared on radio and TV shows in twenty-two cities, coast to coast. I am also on the Tool Advisory Council for Ryobi Tools. From this experience I have gotten a good sampling of the kinds of problems that concern the do-it-yourself homeowner.

We know from do-it-yourselfer statistics that interior home remodeling and maintenance jobs, including patching and painting of walls and ceilings, are the most popular jobs for do-it-yourself homeowners. Statistics estimate that 94 percent of homeowners do at least some of their own interior painting, which includes the usual patching, sanding, and smoothing tasks that precede painting.

So when publisher Robert Hostage and I were seeking a new subject for a book, the subject of floors, walls, and ceilings seemed a most logical title. Our goal is to address the most popular projects undertaken by homeowners, and to provide new and professional insights and techniques for solving those common problems. Our premise is that, no matter what your project, there may be many ways to accomplish it, but there is always a *best* way to do anything, and we will try to tell you that best way.

1
Plaster

Plaster is a combination of gypsum, sand, and lime, mixed with water to form a plastic material that can be troweled over masonry or wood-framed walls. Plaster is used to compensate for uneven framing and to create a smooth and flat interior wall/ceiling system that will accept a variety of interior decorating systems; to fill cracks to stop air infiltration; and to keep out insects and dirt. By increasing the thickness (mass) of plaster, you can increase the sound-proofing and fireproofing values of a wall or ceiling. Plaster was the most common interior finish material for residential housing until well after World War II, when the drywall or wallboard industry gained popularity.

Plaster has always been valued as a premium interior finish that can be used to smooth and flatten irregular framing. But because it is plastic (easy to shape), plaster also is used to form decorative ceiling coves (sort of like plaster molding), round arches, curved walls, and decorative medallions to enhance the ceilings where lighting or chandeliers are mounted.

But plaster has its drawbacks. It is labor intensive to apply and introduces gallons — even barrels — of water into a building. The large quantity of water thus introduced presents at least two problems for the builder. The water will cause wood components of the house to swell or expand, and the subsequent wood shrinkage when the moisture escapes causes warping of the framing lumber and cracking of the plaster. Plus, in humid weather the plaster will cure slowly and will take days or even weeks to give up its water content. This curing time represents lost time to the builder; lost time that is not required if one uses wallboard construction instead of plaster. Because time is money, and plastering takes more time than wallboard construction, plaster gave way to wallboard construction in most residential applications. (New thincoat plaster systems are not only faster to apply than old-style plaster but do not introduce the moisture problems that thicker, conventional plaster did.) In addition to drying time for plaster, builders must wait until the plaster *cures* or hardens before proceeding with other finishing tasks. The vibration from installing flooring or trim will crack plaster that has not cured. This extra waiting period slows the progress of construction and delays completion, so it is an added expense. Thus, when a mature wallboard system was available, most residential builders switched from plaster to wallboard construction, because wallboard construction was both faster and cheaper than wet plaster.

BASICS OF PLASTER CONSTRUCTION

In wet plaster construction, a type of material called *lath* must be applied over the framing members to provide a base for plaster application. This lath may be wood strips, gypsum panels, which are called "rock lath," or a screen-like steel material called "wire lath." To find out which kind of lath was used in your house, remove the covers from electrical outlets or the registers from heating ducts and look

Plaster construction offers a variety of finish options in residential construction. Coved ceilings, fancy archways, and decorative figures or medallions can be included in plaster construction. Photo courtesy of USG.

Plaster requires dexterity and skills that are usually beyond the levels of the do-it-yourselfer. Hire pros to do new plaster work or extensive repairs. Photo courtesy of USG.

at the edges of the plaster around these openings. You should be able to see the type of lath beneath the plaster.

You can also make an educated guess as to which type of lath you have if you know the age of the house. Until the 1940s wood lath was used. After World War II rock lath was developed and replaced wood lath in most residential plaster jobs. Wire lath was the most expensive and was most often used in commercial building or in mansion-class homes. However, you may find some wire lath used to reinforce corners or other areas in wood lath jobs. Wood lath is about 1/4 inch thick and rock or gypsum lath is 3/8 inch thick.

Wood lath is installed with 1/4-inch wide cracks, called keyways, between the wood laths. As the wet plaster is troweled over the laths, the plaster is forced into the keyways between the lath strips and curls behind the lath to form "keys," which hold the plaster tight to the laths. If you have wood lath under your plaster, patching the plaster can be simplified, because the wood lath will hold screws, nails, or staples to help support the patch plaster and hold it until it dries so the patch material cannot sag. Soft rock (gypsum) lath will not support nails or other fasteners, and damaged rock lath must be removed and a new piece of rock lath installed to hold any plaster patch material.

When the plaster lath is in place, a base coat of plaster is applied by trowel or spray pump. This first or base coat of plaster is called the *brown* coat. The brown coat is made by mixing gypsum plaster with sand and water. The brown coat is applied over the lath with an average thickness of 1/2 inch, but a long straightedge, called a *darby*, is used to level the entire surface of the wall or ceiling. The darby helps compensate for warped or crooked framing and may pile plaster much thicker than the average in "low" areas in order to level the surface of the plaster. Before the brown coat is dry, a toothed tool is moved over the surface to create scratches or to roughen or *scarify* the brown coat. These scratches

help create a good bond between the first or brown coat and the second or finish coat of plaster.

When the brown or first plaster coat is dry, a second, smoothing coat of lime is troweled over the entire brown coat plaster area. This finish coat is white, can be troweled to a mirror-like smoothness, and is very hard when cured. This extremely hard finish will resist impact damage and will readily accept any decoration from paint to wall covering.

It is important to understand the preceding basics of plaster construction, so that you can understand the nature of any damage or failure of the plaster. Repair techniques needed will depend on the nature of the damage or failure of the plaster itself.

Most cracks in plaster are *structural*, meaning the crack is caused by movement of the house structure (more about this later).

Water damage or aging, on the other hand, may cause delamination or failure of the bond between the plaster lath and the first (brown) coat, or between the brown coat and the top (lime or finish) coat. To repair loose plaster you must remove only the plaster that is loose, then patch back over the plaster lath or over the first or brown coat.

The final problem you may have to deal with is the complete failure of the plaster when its useful life is ended. When the plaster fails over more than half the total plaster area, only complete renovation will remedy the problem. The plaster must either be totally removed back to the framing, and new plaster or wallboard installed, or (if the plaster is badly deteriorated but still basically tight to the lath), covered over with a new layer or *skin* of wallboard.

PLASTER REPAIR: CRACKS

When cured, plaster achieves a brittle hardness, not unlike panes of glass. When the house settles or loses moisture from construction, there is unavoidable shrinkage of the framing members — wall studs and ceiling or floor joists — and this framing shrinkage causes stress in the brittle plaster. This stress is most common at or near the center of the plaster ceiling, and is perpendicular to the ceiling joists, so any ceiling crack that occurs at the center of the ceiling, and extends for the full length of the ceiling, is due to flexing or shrinking of the ceiling joists. Other common stress/crack points in plaster occur at corners where ceilings meet walls or walls meet walls. These cracks occur because the wood framing members in the ceiling, the ceiling joists, shrink in one direction, while the wood in the top wall plates shrinks in the opposite direction, thus pulling the plaster apart and causing a crack. This same effect, in which opposing framing members shrink in opposite directions, causes the cracks at corners where walls meet walls, or at the headers above doors and windows, when jackstuds or cripple studs shrink in opposite directions and pull the plaster apart, cracking it.

These plaster cracks, caused by movement of the framing or structure, are called *structural* cracks. They cannot be repaired by filling them with spackle or with patch plaster, because the underlying cause, the movement of the framing or structure, will recur any time the temperature and/or humidity change. You must reinforce structural cracks with fiberglass patches or with wallboard tape to prevent them from cracking again.

Plaster patching kits that contain fiberglass cloth and resin can be used to patch structural cracks. To use these plaster repair kits just follow the directions on the kit.

To patch a structural crack with wallboard joint tape, use the fiber or paper (not pre-glued fiberglass tape) and ready-mixed taping compound. Using a 6-inch taping knife, apply the taping compound directly over the plaster crack, then embed the fiber wallboard tape in the compound. Use the 6-inch taping knife to press the excess taping compound from underneath the fiber tape. Immediately cover the smoothed tape with a *thin* skim coat of taping compound. Let the patch dry, then apply another *thin* coat of taping compound over the tape and let dry.

Notice we emphasize that covering coats of compound that are over the taped crack should be thin or skim coats; if you pile taping compound over the crack this heavy layer of taping compound will itself crack when the wall structure moves. Keep the total thickness of the patch at a minimum to prevent future surface cracks. When the wallboard compound is dry, use a wet sponge to smooth the patch, then spot prime with primer or a coat of latex paint. Let the primer coat dry, then decorate to suit.

Most repair texts make a point of distinguishing between *structural* cracks and *hairline* cracks. To the professional plasterer a hairline crack is a minor crack that may be caused by shrinkage in the plaster material that occurs during the curing process. If you have small hairline cracks that do not extend over a wide portion of the wall, observe the cracks as the seasons or temperature and humidity change. If the cracks do not vary in size as conditions change, the cracks are hairline and can be repaired by filling them with patch plaster or spackle. When in doubt, and always when redecorating, treat any cracks as structural and reinforce them with fiberglass or wallboard tape. This way, crack repair will be permanent and you won't have cracks recurring in six months, spoiling your new decorating job.

PLASTER REPAIR: HOLES

Check any holes in plaster to see if they extend through the lath, to the lath, or only through the top or lime coat. Be sure to remove any cracked or loose plaster before proceeding with the repair.

If the lath is intact, you need only to fill the hole with patch plaster and smooth it. If the lath is damaged, you can insert new lath or cut a piece of wire lath and insert it in the hole. You must anchor the wire lath in place with nails or staples (if there is wood underneath, either wood lath or framing, to support the fasteners) or with hot-melt glue from a glue gun. You must have lath in place to prevent the patch plaster from sagging or falling out of the hole.

If the lath is intact, or when you have installed new lath, use a small paint brush to coat the lath and the edges of the old plaster with a latex concrete/plaster bonder. This bonder is a white latex that resembles white wood glue. The bonder prevents the old dry lath and plaster from absorbing the water from the patching plaster, causing premature drying and cracking of the new patch material, and it ensures a bond between the old lath/plaster and the new patching material. Ask your dealer for Quikrete's Concrete Bonding Adhesive or an equivalent product.

While the bonding adhesive is still sticky, mix the patch plaster according to label directions. Use a wallboard taping knife or trowel to apply the patching plaster in the hole and to smooth it. One common error of how-to texts is to show a patching tool that is not wide enough to span the repair area. For any hole less than 6 inches wide, use a 6-inch wallboard knife to smooth the hole. For any hole less than 12 inches wide use a plastering trowel or wide wallboard finishing knife to make the repair. The point is that the wider tool will ride on the edges of the repair hole, using these edges as a guide for filling the hole. Using a narrow patching tool will result in a patch that is rough and not even or level to the top of the hole.

If the hole to be patched is more than $1/2$ inch deep, fill the hole about halfway, let it set hard, then fill the hole to the top, level with the existing plaster. If the hole is less than $1/2$ inch deep, apply and smooth the patching plaster in one application. Use fine sandpaper or a wet sponge to smooth the repair area, then spot prime and decorate as preferred. If the hole to be patched is wider than a plasterer's trowel (about 12 inches wide) use the trowel to fill the hole with plaster, then use a straightedge such as an aluminum yardstick to level and smooth the patch.

PLASTER FAILURE

Plaster can last virtually forever, but its useful life depends on the quality of the material used. Plaster that contains a high percentage of sand will be softer than plaster that has a higher gypsum/sand ratio. In time plaster will fail and must be repaired or replaced.

If plaster has become loose from the lath over a limited area it can sometimes be salvaged. This judgment should be made by a professional. If the plaster is loose from wood lath, large-headed plaster screws can be used to tie the plaster back to the lath and replace the "keys" (curled plaster between the laths) that have failed. Use a screw such as USG's Durock wood screw, available from suppliers of drywall or plaster products. Look in the Yellow Pages under Building Materials for a supplier. The screwheads and any cracks in the plaster can then be covered over with patching compound (either plaster or taping compound).

There is also a plaster repair technique that involves injecting an adhesive in the space between the loose plaster and the lath. This must be done by a professional. For more information contact: Adhesive Engineering/Harry S. Peterson, Inc., 1411 Industrial Rd., San Carlos, CA 94070.

Other plaster replacement methods are available and can be done by an accomplished do-it-yourselfer. These methods vary depending on whether the surface to be replaced is a ceiling, a wall, or both. Because of problems with trim, window/door jamb extensions, and heating/electrical outlets, renewing plaster walls is more difficult than renewing plaster ceilings.

Before making a decision to cover or replace plaster completely, make your own inspection of the plaster surface. Obvious signs of plaster failure include wide and/or extensive cracks, holes where plaster is already missing, or visible bulging that indicates the plaster is separated from the lath.

If plaster is cracked or there are holes, or the plaster surface is obviously bulged or uneven, press with the flat of your hand against the damaged area. Move your hand, pressing as you go, along the crack lines, on both sides, to see if the plaster is only cracked (which can be repaired) or is loose from the lath over a substantial area. Press against any bulges or uneven areas to see if the plaster is "spongy" and loose from the lath. If the affected area is small, the loose plaster can be removed and the missing area filled and leveled. If the plaster is loose from the lath over more than half the ceiling or wall area, complete removal and replacement, or coverup, will be necessary.

CEILINGS

If plaster has failed over all or most of the ceiling area, ignoring it can be dangerous: plaster is heavy, and large chunks that fall can do serious injury to residents. Don't ignore loose plaster, especially on wood lath, because the entire plaster ceiling can drop at once when plaster keys between the laths fail. Plaster over wire lath or over gypsum or rock lath will not fail over so wide an area unless there is extensive damage from water or other sources.

Failing plaster ceilings can be left in place and covered over with wallboard. If the plaster is still flat and level, only badly broken or cracked, you can install wallboard directly over the old plaster, using a screw gun and wallboard screws. Use an electronic stud finder or a nail and hammer in a trial-and-error pattern. (See Chapter 9 for how to find studs and joists in walls and ceilings.) Install the wallboard panels so they are perpendicular to, not parallel with, the ceiling joists.

Be sure the wallboard screws are long enough to penetrate through the 1/2-inch thickness of the wallboard, plus the 3/4-inch thickness (average) of the plaster, plus penetrating into the joists by at least 3/4 inch (a total screw length of 2 inches or more).

In most cases you should install furring strips (1 x 2s) over the plaster, then install wallboard panels, using wallboard screws to secure the wallboard to the furring strips. Note that you can install 3/4-inch thick panels of Styrofoam insulation board between the furring strips for better ceiling insulation, which will add about 4-R to the ceiling insulation value.

To install furring strips on the ceiling, plan to nail 1 x 2 strips perpendicular to the existing joists, using 8d nails to reach through the furring strips, through the 3/4-inch thick plaster, and into the ceiling joists. Temporarily nail the furring strips in place, and check the ceiling for level. Use cedar shingles as shims to level the furring strips as you go, so the new strips will be absolutely level. Install the Styrofoam insulation boards between the furring strips. Then install the 1/2-inch thick wallboard panels over the furring strips, using 1-inch long wallboard screws to fasten the panels to the strips. (See Chapter 2, Hanging Wallboard, for more information.) Finish the wallboard and spray or paint the ceiling as desired.

WALLS

Although it can be done, covering old plaster walls with a new wallboard "skin" is more difficult than covering old plaster ceilings. To do a first class job of covering old walls, you should remove all existing trim, extend the jambs on the window and door frames, then use wallboard screws to install new 3/8-inch thick wallboard panels over the old plaster. Then finish the wallboard, prime and/or paint it, then reinstall the old trim. To extend existing jambs means to install nailer strips (usually ripped pine boards) on the edges of the jambs to bring them flush with the new wall surface. For example, if you removed the trim and installed 3/8-inch thick wallboard over the old plaster, you would rip 3/8-inch thick pine strips and nail them on the faces of the jambs so the new trim would be flush with the new wallboard.

Note that the suggestions for covering old plaster are intended to help you get a new surface on walls or ceilings by installing wallboard/furring and wallboard over the old plaster, leaving the plaster in place. This will save a lot of hard work, dirt and dust, and plaster disposal. It will also let you (in the ceiling example) leave any existing insulation in place on the ceiling, saving the work of removing/replacing the insulation.

In addition to extending the door and window jambs, you must also extend the electrical receptacles out to meet the new wall surfaces. Adding a new layer of wallboard and extending the outlets may also mean that the electrical wires are too short to reach the outlets when they are fitted on the surface of the wallboard. This would mean that the walls would have to be rewired.

Old plaster that is sound and still tight to the lath, but has many hairline cracks or small blemishes, can be covered over with wall covering. Years ago, in upper bracket houses, plaster walls were routinely covered with white wall covering, usually canvas (called "blank stock") before the decorators came in with their paint or wallpaper. The canvas on the plaster prevented small blemishes or hairline cracks from showing through the finish paint or wallpaper, and paperhangers can still "canvas" walls to conceal minor problems.

PANELING

Installing wood paneling over the old plaster is another possibility. Certainly one would not want to panel the whole house: this approach, common in the '50s, became widely known as "remuddling." Many people who admire the style and charm of old houses think such paneling was an abomination. Often, these really bad paneling jobs were done by amateurs, using the cheapest paneling available, and did indeed ruin the interior of a house.

But, properly done and using quality materials, wood paneling can both provide decorative appeal and cover up for failing plaster. A dining room, library, family room, or foyer can be done in wood paneling and can add to the value and visual appeal of the house. The point is that you must use quality materials and execute the job in a workmanlike manner. Poor materials and/or poor workmanship will doom any project to failure.

There are times when you will want to gut the house, removing the old plaster and lath down to the bare studs. This would be necessary if you were doing a complete modernization of your house, upgrading the electrical system, insulation, and ventilation to meet today's standards. Then complete removal of the old plaster is the best approach, since you must open up all wall and ceiling cavities to full access.

2
Hanging Wallboard

Various types of wallboard have been around for more than a half century. Gypsum panels were available as far back as the 1920s, but no specific system of tape and compound had been developed for finishing the wallboard. Wallboard or drywall construction, including a system for finishing the joints and corners, came into widespread use to meet the emergency housing needs during World War II. Because a worldwide depression and a world war consumed the resources of the nation during the decades of the '30s and '40s, there was virtually no residential construction in the U.S. throughout that period. Thus, a residential building boom began following the war, in the latter half of the 1940s. This residential housing boom saw the emergence of tract building of houses to meet the pent-up housing demand, and wallboard or drywall construction, which was both faster and cheaper than plaster construction, became a new industry. Within a few years wallboard construction became the standard of the building industry, and a majority of new homes had wallboard as an interior finish.

When compared to the skills and labor involved in installing wet plaster, nailing on gypsum wallboard panels and treating the joints with compound is an amateur's dream, so wallboard quickly became a popular material for the do-it-yourselfer. But acres of badly installed and poorly finished wallboard across the country confirm the fact that a certain level of knowledge and skill is needed for performing a quality wallboard installation job. Even though

there is a massive flow of d-i-y information, via how-to magazines, books such as this one, and instructional video tapes, there is still much erroneous and outdated how-to information floating about. Working from the theory that there is a best way to do anything, we'll try to reject outdated advice and instead suggest the best materials, tools, and techniques for working with wallboard.

First, a few personal observations. I started working with wallboard in the summer of 1947 and learned the trade from my father. At that time $3/8$-inch thick wallboard was commonly being used in new houses. This lightweight material soon yielded to the stronger $1/2$-inch thick panels and today $5/8$-inch thick panels are standard for use on ceilings or in other areas where framing is spaced 24 inches on center.

In those early days we used 5d cc (cement coated) nails or blued (plaster) lath nails to install the wallboard. But someone used blued lath nails in a new house that was being built for a certain building inspector. Lath nails had oversized heads, and when you hit the nail heads off center the edges of the nail head would curl under and cut through the face paper of the wallboard. These nails would "pop" and show an unsightly bulge or dent at each nail location. The inspector, disgusted at having popped nails throughout the wallboard in his new home, decreed that lath nails would be forbidden by housing code for wallboard installation. We then began to use the 5d nails only, while the wallboard industry searched for a better fastener.

One early improvement in fasteners was the "cupped" or "bugle head" wallboard nail. The cupped head could be driven below the face of the wallboard without fracturing the face paper around the nail head. Then came ring-shank nails, which had better holding power than smooth-shanked nails. Finally the wallboard screw, combined with wallboard adhesives, became the ultimate method for fastening wallboard. Can you still use nails to install wallboard? Of course you can, but you are using the technologies of the 1950s. Screw or screw/adhesive installation of wallboard is by far the best, for reasons we hope will become apparent.

In those early days we had only one type of finish compound, and it was equivalent to the taping compound of today. Then the industry perfected a "topping" compound that did not contain enough adhesive to be used for applying the wallboard tape, but could be troweled smoother and sanded more easily than taping compound. Then we began to use the new topping compound for the second and third coats, for better workability and a better finished job.

Later, a ready-mixed, all-purpose wallboard compound was developed. This permitted one to use only one taping compound instead of fussing about with several different materials (the compound you need is the one you are out of) and also to avoid the mistakes one can make when mixing the powder type of taping compound. Pros may choose, for a variety of reasons, to use the powder-type taping compound available in 25-pound bags. But the best choice of taping compound for the d-i-y'er is the all-purpose, ready-mixed compound available in one-gallon or five-gallon plastic pails.

In those early days no metal corner beads were available for finishing outside corners. The finishing method for outside corners was to fold wallboard tape and "soft tape" the corners. Within a few years one could buy all-steel, nail-on corner beads, or glue-on (with adhesive) fiber tape corner beads that have an aluminum angle at the center. For the d-i-y'er the best choice for corner bead is the all-steel,

nail-on corner bead. If you have outside corners that are not square, or 90 degrees, buy the flex-bead corners that can be folded to match any angle and are installed using taping compound as an adhesive.

One drawback to using wallboard in remodeling jobs is that powder-type (mixed with water) or ready-mix vinyl taping compounds require twenty-four hours for drying time between coats, even under ideal drying conditions. This results in a delay of three to four days to do even small wallboard jobs. But quick-drying taping compounds have been developed that "set" or harden like plaster, rather than air-drying as ordinary taping compounds do. The quick-set compounds must be mixed with water and used within a short period of time — two hours or less — so you must mix only enough to last for the set time listed on the bag. However, the d-i-y'er may choose to use these quick-set materials in order to complete a small job in one work day, with no waiting period between coats to delay the job progress.

Our purpose in reviewing all the materials available is to reinforce our first premise: there is a right way, or at least a best way, to do anything, including wallboard installation. It is a disservice to the reader to suggest using any but the best techniques and materials for doing your project.

BUYING WALLBOARD

Wallboard is made in factories, where wet gypsum plaster is pressed between two sheets of paper, forming panels of various thicknesses and lengths. Wallboard is available in thicknesses of 1/4 inch (must be special ordered), 3/8 inch, 1/2 inch, and 5/8 inch. Keep in mind that each 1/8-inch increase of thickness increases the weight, strength, and stiffness of the wallboard panel, because the extra thickness is made of pure plaster. The thickness of wallboard you will use depends on the job to be done. Quarter-inch thick wallboard has little strength and is used only as a covering layer or new "skin" or face surface over an existing plaster wall.

Panels of $3/8$-inch thick wallboard are not strong or stiff enough to be used alone for single-layer wallboard interiors, but $3/8$-inch thick panels can be used as an underlayment or a base material for installing wall paneling. To get a laminated wallboard system that has the same fireproofing and soundproofing qualities of plaster, with the economy and speed of construction of wallboard, use two layers of $3/8$-inch thick wallboard. In laminated wallboard construction, the first layer of $3/8$-inch thick panels is nailed to the framing, parallel to the studs or joists. Then a second layer of $3/8$-inch thick wallboard is adhesively applied over the first layer of wallboard, with the second-layer wallboard panels applied at right angles or perpendicular to the framing. If you remove old plaster down to bare framing, you can match the old plaster thickness of $3/4$ inch, and thus match the thickness of the existing door and window frames, by installing a double or laminated layer of $3/8$-inch thick wallboard to make a total finished wall or ceiling thickness of $3/4$ inch.

The standard of the wallboard industry, for use on residential housing with framing set 16 inches o.c. (on center), is the $1/2$-inch thick wallboard panel. The majority of houses built in the past forty years have walls and ceilings of $1/2$-inch thick wallboard, and this thickness is even approved for use on framing up to 24 inches o.c. However, because of the extra ceiling insulation requirements for today's energy conservation, you should use $5/8$-inch thick wallboard over 24-inch o.c. framing, such as on ceiling trusses set on 24-inch centers, to handle the extra insulation weight.

Thicker $5/8$-inch thick wallboard is also used where superior fireproofing is needed. For example, $5/8$-inch thick wallboard (sometimes called $5/8$" Firecode) is required by building codes in firewalls or ceilings between attached garages or between multiple residential units, such as for firewalls between condominium or townhouse units. This thicker $5/8$-inch wallboard has a 60-minute fire rating, as opposed to a 45-minute fire rating for $1/2$-inch thick wallboard. The fire rating is expressed as the number of min-

utes it will take for a fire on one side of the partition to kindle the framing members inside the wall and spread the fire to the next room or living unit.

Note that you can increase the fire rating of a wall or ceiling by using multiple layers of wallboard panels: two layers of $5/8$-inch thick wallboard, glued or screwed to a wall or ceiling, will provide twice the fire rating of the single panel, or two hours rating rather than the 60-minute fire rating of the single panel. The same thing is true for soundproofing a wall or ceiling: the more layers of wallboard or the greater the thickness, the greater the mass or weight of the wall or ceiling, and the greater the resistance to sound transfer.

Gypsum wallboard can also be used for exterior applications that are not directly exposed to rain or weather, such as inside unheated garage space or for soffits or porch ceilings. The exterior wallboard application should be done during warm weather, so that taping compound used for finishing joints and nail or screw heads will not freeze. The exterior wallboard should be painted with two coats, using an exterior grade of latex or acrylic paint.

The second thing you must decide is the length of wallboard to use. Walls can flash or shadow through the paint, and joints can crack and ruin the appearance of the job. All wallboard manufacturers (and the Gypsum Association) agree that you should use the longest panels possible to reduce the number of joints in the job. This means that the best job is one that uses 12-foot long panels, on both walls and ceilings, with the 12-foot panels installed perpendicular to the framing. If you are doing a job in which the rooms are all less than 8 feet square (closets, new hallways, etc.), you would buy 8-foot long wallboard panels, because the longer 12-foot panels cannot be used. And, if you are finishing off an attic or basement room(s) and stair access is so limited that you cannot carry longer panels into the area, then you would have no choice but to use the shorter 8-foot long panels. But with these exceptions the *best* wallboard job, with the fewest joints, can be gotten by using the longest wallboard panels available or 12-foot long panels. Nor is the claim that the shorter 8-foot wallboard panels are "lighter and easier for the homeowner to handle" an intelligent argument for using shorter panels. The panels will be installed only once, but you will have to look at and live with the job for years to come. Don't settle for an inferior job just for ease of application. If you don't have a helper, or installing the longer (and heavier) 12-foot panels seems too difficult for you, by all means have this work done by professionals.

INSTALLING WALLBOARD

Scaffold

To install wallboard you will need a suitable scaffold or sawhorses and planks to let you comfortably reach the ceiling. Most people who attempt wallboard work try to install ceiling panels while using odd-sized sawhorses or planks and ladders — any odd scaffold that is available — to reach ceilings. Working on scaffold of the wrong height, while handling heavy and awkward wallboard panels, is hard and tiring work. Handling the weight of wallboard while stretching upward or crouching down to match the scaffold height will quickly tire you out and convince you that installing wallboard is hard work. Build proper scaffold to help you reach ceilings comfortably and safely.

The ideal scaffold for installing ceiling wallboard is a pair of sawhorses built to fit the height of the workers and the height of the ceiling. Assuming you will apply wallboard to a ceiling of traditional 8-foot height, you should subtract your own height from 8 feet, and build a sawhorse that height. For example, if you are 6 feet tall, and will be hanging wallboard on an 8-foot ceiling, build your sawhorse 24 inches or 2 feet tall. Then, suppose your helper is 5'6" or 66 inches tall. You would subtract 66 inches from 96 inches (the 8-foot ceiling height) and build the helper's sawhorse 30 inches tall. Using a 2 x 12 for a scaffold plank, and being sure

each worker is careful to work his/her own end of the scaffold (the end that fits your own size and not your partner's), each worker can hold the wallboard panel atop his/her head, using the head for a "third hand" to hold the panel firmly against the ceiling joists while leaving the hands free for screwing the panel to the framing. Caution: Place a sponge in a cap and wear the cap while using the head to hold up the wallboard, to avoid a real "Excedrin headache."

Many texts suggest using "props," or 2 x 4s nailed in a "T" shape, to hold the wallboard panels against the ceiling. As an ex-professional who did this kind of work for twenty-five years, I never found the use of a prop to be an advantage. My theory is, if you have a free hand to reach for and position the prop, why not just nail or screw the panel in place, rather than propping it? It is much easier to build the scaffold to a comfortable working height, hold the panel up with your head, and fasten it in place.

An option, and one I have personally tried, is to rent a wallboard (drywall) lifter. The lifter is a device that has a pair of arms on which the wallboard panel is placed. Then the lifting wheel on the side of the device is turned and the wallboard panel is raised into position against the ceiling joists. You can then attach the wallboard, using wallboard screws (or nails) at your leisure. I much prefer working with a partner, and using scaffold specifically built for the job, to any other technique, but I prefer using the wallboard lifter to trying to work with clumsy and awkward 2 x 4 props. Props are a pain, especially when one slips and drops a 100-pound wallboard panel on your head. Ignore any advice to use 2 x 4 props to install wallboard on ceilings; either find a helper to help hang the wallboard properly or have the job done by professionals.

Wallboard Installation Tools

After building proper scaffold for hanging the wallboard on ceilings, assemble the tools for wallboard installation. You will need a wallboard screw gun for driving wallboard screws. If you have a very small wallboard installation job and do not own an

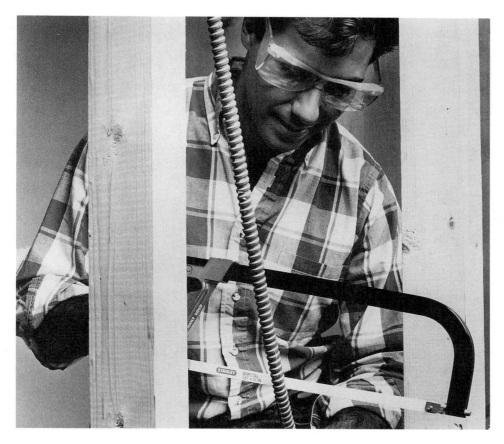

Check framing for alignment and be sure all wiring and plumbing are in place before you begin to install wallboard. Photo courtesy of Stanley Tools.

Use a try-square or combination square for marking ducts and electrical outlets. Use a wallboard T-square for most measuring and cutting operations. Photo courtesy of Stanley Tools.

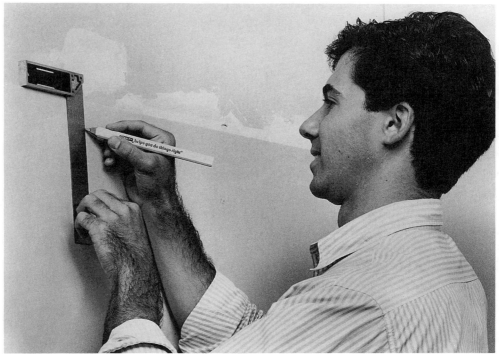

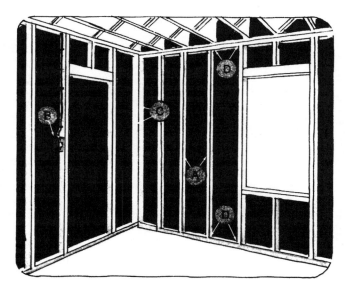

Start with proper framing. (A) Be sure studs are straight. (B) Align all electrical outlets, heating ducts, etc., so they will be flush with finished wallboard surface. (C) Provide nailing surfaces on both sides of vertical corners and headers for all fixtures. (D) Nailing faces on all studs must be flush and in alignment with top and bottom plate faces. Shim where necessary.

electric screw gun, you can use wallboard nails, but nails are an inferior fastener for this purpose. Remember, we promised to tell you the *best* way to do the job, and the best way is to use screws and wallboard adhesives.

Using electric screw guns and screws offers numerous advantages when compared to using a wallboard hammer and nails. Using an impact tool or a hammer can result in damage to the wallboard when the hammer head misses the nail and hits the wallboard. If the driven nail hits a knot in the framing, you may bend it or drive it with excessive force, again damaging the wallboard around the nail head. By the same token, if you attempt to drive a nail into soft wood you may overdrive the nail and make too deep a dimple in the wallboard. If this happens, you may crush the plaster core of the wallboard and destroy the holding power of the nail. Or the hammer face may cut or fracture the face paper around the nail, and these small paper fractures will show through the paint after you begin decorating.

Cut face paper against a straightedge, scoring the gypsum core in preparation for snapping.

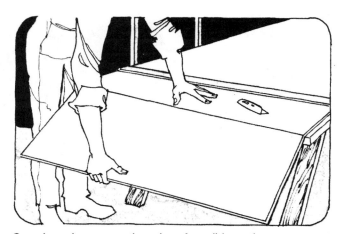

Snap board core over the edge of a solid, continuous support.

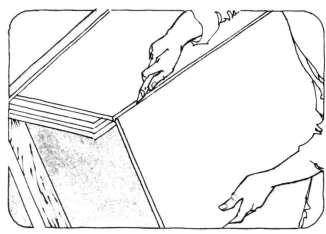

Cut back paper from above or by an upward cut from below.

If no horizontal work surface is available, board can be cut in vertical position as shown.

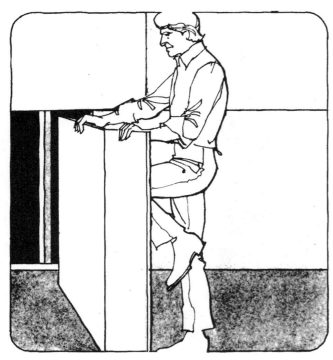

Knee front surface to break back paper.

Using a hammer is also tiring for the worker. The repeated stress that the hammer blows transmit to the wrist and elbow joints can cause tendinitis or "tennis elbow." There is also the "purple thumb" syndrome: you don't hit your thumb when using a wallboard screw gun.

There are also places in the house where nailing is difficult because of the impact and vibration caused by hammering in the nails. Examples would be trying to nail wallboard on lightweight 1 x 4 nailers in soffits, or in the 1 x 4s used in pocket or sliding doors. Longer wallboard nails may penetrate completely through the wallboard and the 1 x 4 nailer in a pocket door, protruding on the inside and scratching or damaging the veneer on the door. Shorter 1-inch long wallboard screws will not penetrate into the door pocket, and screws can be driven into 1 x 4s without causing the vibration that occurs with hammering.

But the single best reason for using a screw gun and wallboard screws is that the shorter (1-inch long) screws have more holding power than wallboard nails, and are less prone to popping than nails, so you simply will have a better job if you use screws than if you use nails to attach the wallboard. The automatic clutch on the screw gun will drive every screw to a preset uniform depth, so all screws will be dimpled equally and will be easy to conceal by applying three coats of taping compound. By contrast, nails are set unevenly, because the nail may penetrate deeper if you hit it harder, or if you are driving the nail into a soft spot in the wood.

In addition to the screw gun, you will need a carpenter's pencil or crayon for marking locations of joists, studs, electrical outlets, and heating ductwork. A sharp number 2 lead pencil can be used for marking the wallboard panels for cutting.

Use a wallboard keyhole saw (it has a straight handle rather than a pistol-grip handle) or a saber saw with a coarse blade for cutting openings in the wallboard. The plaster core of wallboard is highly abrasive and will quickly dull a carpenter's saw.

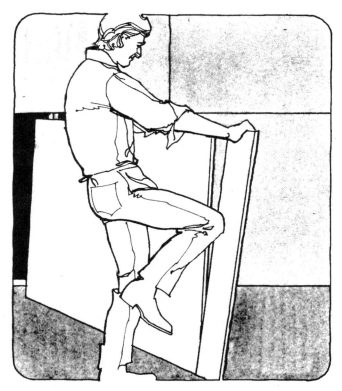

Knee back surface opposite scoring to snap.

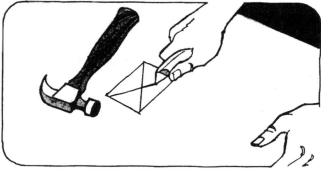

To accommodate electrical outlet boxes, measure for exact location, score proper size rectangle, and score diagonally.

Knock out scored segments with hammer.

Buy a wallboard saw for cutting wallboard. The wallboard saw has larger teeth than a carpenter's wood saw, and the larger teeth will cut quickly through the plaster core without clogging.

You will also need a razor knife and a supply of replacement blades for cutting wallboard. The plaster core will quickly dull the knife blade, and you should replace the blades frequently to ensure a clean cut. Dull blades are also dangerous to the worker, because dull blades can slip when forced, cutting the worker.

Buy a wallboard T-square for marking and cutting wallboard to length. Professional hangers just use the T-square as a cutting guide, rather than marking the cut line and then cutting along the line. The T-square enables you to make a square cut each time for good accuracy. To avoid cutting yourself with a slipped knife, hold the T-square in the desired location, put the toe of your shoe against the bottom leg of the T-square to hold it from slipping, then use a razor knife to cut from the top down, within a foot of your shoe. Then turn the knife over and cut from the bottom edge up to complete the cut. This method eliminates cutting near your foot, where a slipped knife could injure you.

Use a wallboard lifter or a prybar placed on the floor to lift the bottom panel up against the bottom edge of the top panel. You can use a scrap of wood placed under the prybar as a fulcrum if necessary to gain lifting height.

Also a good idea is to buy a carpenter's leather tool belt and pouches to carry the tools and wallboard screws. The tool pouches keep the tools at hand, within easy reach, and eliminate the constant search for tools laid down on the job.

Wear sturdy clothes when working with wallboard. A work cap not only pads the head so you can use your head to support wallboard panels on ceilings, the bill of the cap will help keep the dust from the plaster core out of your eyes. Jeans are tough, resist snagging when you are climbing, and help protect the skin from scrapes and cuts. A long-sleeved shirt can be buttoned at wrists and neck to keep out fiberglass insulation and plaster dust. Always be aware of the danger of puncture wounds to feet from stray nails or boards with nails in them. Wear work shoes with heavy soles and high ankle support around a construction site.

Checking Out the Job

Wet plaster is spread over the lath using a straight-edge or darby, so plaster can be used to make a level wall or ceiling over uneven framing. Wallboard panels are of uniform thickness, and will bend when fastened to meet crooked framing, so the finished wall or ceiling will be only as straight as the framing lumber to which it is attached. It is therefore impor-tant to check out the area to be covered by wallboard and be sure all framing is in place and straight before installing the panels.

To check the framing, first select a straightedge at least 6 feet long — long enough to span at least four studs or joists on 16-inch centers when held perpen-dicular to the framing. Start at any corner and place the straightedge perpendicular to the studs or joists. Check the alignment of the framing, and mark any stud or joist that is bowed or twisted, or out of alignment relative to the other framing members. Use a carpenter's crayon or pencil to mark any stud or joist that is "high" or misaligned relative to its neighbors. When you have checked the alignment of all the wall studs and/or ceiling joists, and marked those that are badly out of alignment, go back over the room and plan the layout of the wallboard.

First, let us agree on terminology. Some people refer to a framing member — either a stud or joist — as being "high" if the face or front edge of the stud or joist is *nearer* to the worker than its neighbors on either side. In this text any reference to a "high" joist or stud means that the bottom of the joist or front edge of the stud is *farther away* from the worker than are its neighbors.

Start with ceiling application, length of board at right angles to joists. If possible, span the entire width of the ceiling with single lengths. Use temporary bracing.

Upper sidewall panel is applied next, abutting ceiling. Nailing begins near the center of the board and proceeds toward ends.

Wallboard is easy to cut, using a razor knife. Replace knife blades frequently to keep blade sharp. Keep free hand and legs away from the knife to avoid a cut if knife slips. Photo courtesy of Gold Bond.

Industrial Drywall Screwdriver has positive depth adjustment, magnetic bit to hold wallboard screws, and removable belt clip. Photo courtesy of Sears.

Lower sidewall panel is held snugly but not forcibly against the upper panel. A simply contrived, foot-operated lever will position the panel until several nails are driven to hold board in place.

Window cutouts are sometimes made after wallboard is in place. Saw cut is flush against rough frame. Vertical cuts are sawed; horizontal cut is scored and snapped.

Knee wall finishing is essentially the same as for regular walls. Edge of lower panel is butted firmly but not forcibly against the edge of the upper panel. End joints of upper and lower panels should be staggered (upper panel in drawing is cut back to show framing).

Multi-flex tape with dual metal ribbons is well suited to knee wall joint treatment. Metal side faces the wall. Joint compound is applied in the same manner as for regular paper joint tape. Illustrations courtesy of Gold Bond.

Keep in mind that there are several ways to correct problems with framing alignment. In many cases you can remove warped or crooked studs and replace them with straight studs. Obviously, it is easier to replace warped studs on an interior wall than to replace studs on exterior walls where wall sheathing is nailed to the studs and makes removal difficult. For removing studs on interior walls, just use a carpenter's hammer, striking at both stud ends where the stud is nailed to the top and sole 2 x 4 plates to knock out the warped studs, and then toenail new studs into place.

Nailing is a poor second as a method for hanging wallboard: always use wallboard screws on large jobs. For minor projects, if you choose to use a hammer, buy a hammer designed for wallboard application. Photo courtesy of USG.

Another good method for straightening a crooked wall or ceiling is to apply wallboard or stud adhesives in a strategic pattern on the framing when installing wallboard. For example, we can apply a larger bead of adhesive to one stud than we apply to other studs, and thus help correct the alignment. Or if we have a stud that is "high," we can apply stud adhesive to that stud and none to the stud on either side. By applying an adhesive bead of up to 3/8 inch in diameter we can thus use the adhesive to "furr out" up to 3/8-inch misalignment.

If you are applying wallboard to a basement ceiling and find that the joists are misaligned, you cannot easily remove and replace warped joists. Instead, it is best to cut filler strips or shims out of 1/4-inch paneling or plywood, or to cut shim strips from asphalt shingles. Place the straightedge over a series of joists, and nail either plywood or asphalt shingle shims to the "high" joists.

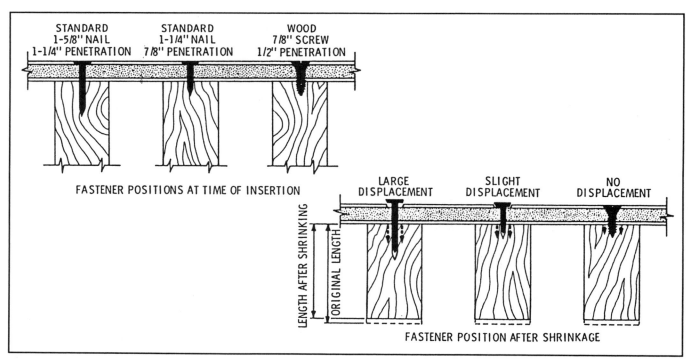

If you use fasteners that are too long, you may get fastener failures or nail pops. The main causes of nail pops are wet lumber and oversized (too long) fasteners. The degree of pop will depend on the shrinkage in the wood that is penetrated by the fastener.

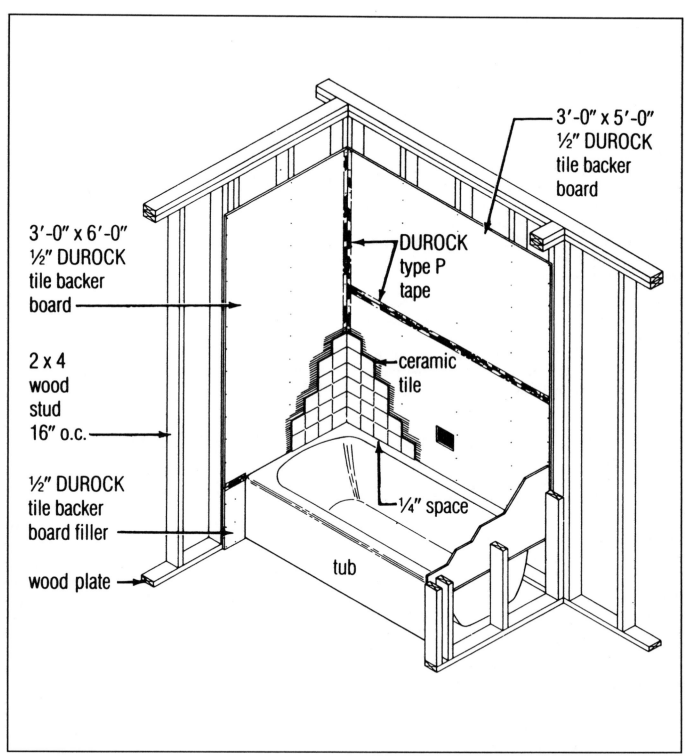

3'-0" x 5'-0"
½" DUROCK
tile backer
board

DUROCK
type P
tape

3'-0" x 6'-0"
½" DUROCK
tile backer
board

2 x 4
wood
stud
16" o.c.

ceramic
tile

½" DUROCK
tile backer
board filler

¼" space

wood plate

tub

Rather than using wallboard, use a cement product such as USG's Durock as a base for ceramic tile. Courtesy of USG.

When you have checked and corrected framing alignment, check for other obstructions that may interfere with wallboard installation. Check at corners to be sure there is backing or nailers at all corners to support the wallboard ends. If there is bridging between the joists (as in a basement ceiling) check the ends of the bridging to be sure they do not extend below the bottom of the joists. If the bridging is wood, use a carpenter's saw to cut off the tip of the bridging that extends below the joist bottom edge, because it will interfere with wallboard placement. If the bridging is metal, you may be able to drive the end of the bridging above the edge of the joist, using a hammer, or you may have to remove and reposition the metal bridging.

Be sure all wiring and plumbing are in place, and check the electrical outlet boxes to be sure they are set in the right position; i.e., the front edge of the outlet box should be flush with the face of the installed wallboard. This means the outlet boxes should protrude $1/2$ inch beyond the front edge of the studs if you will install $1/2$-inch thick wallboard, or protrude $5/8$ inch beyond the framing for $5/8$-inch wallboard. Nail metal protector plates over studs where water pipes are routed through framing, to prevent wallboard screws or nails from penetrating into the water pipes, causing plumbing leaks in your new wall or ceiling.

Check also to be sure all insulation is in place, both for energy conservation and for soundproofing. Insulating the walls between a bathroom and living areas, for example, can reduce transmission of embarrassing noises through the partition. Also, install a vapor barrier over ceiling and outside walls, and check to be sure the vapor barrier has not been ripped by careless workmen before covering the vapor barrier with the wallboard panels.

For new construction, use the carpenter's crayon to mark the position of the studs on the subfloor plywood. Also, mark the position of the ceiling joists or trusses on the top plate of all walls, so you can easily locate the joists or trusses for screwing on the wallboard.

Aluminum bench for hanging wallboard folds for easy transport and storage. Available at professional wallboard supply stores or from rental outlets. Courtesy Wal-Board Tools.

Planning for Butt (End) Joints

A common warning in consumer "how-to" texts is to install 4-foot x 8-foot wallboard panels parallel to the studs on walls, thus avoiding the dreaded butt joints, which are universally proclaimed to be "very difficult to finish." This, of course, is nonsense. If you visit a new home under construction you will see that professional installers install 12-foot long wallboard panels, and install them perpendicular or at right angles to the studs or joists. This method of application reduces the total footage of joints to be finished by at least 25 percent; it makes the joints easier to conceal; and it makes a much stronger wall or ceiling, for reasons we will discuss later. But when you install wallboard perpendicular to the framing, you will have butt joints on any wall or ceiling that is longer than 12 feet. Wallboard finishers must routinely finish butt or end joints and do so successfully. The key is to plan butt joint placement and construction very carefully, and do not create a butt joint that is impossible to conceal.

One point to keep in mind from the outset: amateurs measure from a corner and position the butt joint on the joist or stud that occurs nearest the end of the wallboard panel. To build a good butt joint, you may decide to move to a new stud or joist and place the butt joint there. You can start measuring from the opposite wall, so the butt joint will occur on another stud or joist. Or you can shim the joists on either side of the butt joint with wallboard adhesive to "shim" the joists into alignment. Or you can use the pro's technique of "floating" the butt joint between the studs or joists.

The key to creating a good butt joint is to check the framing carefully as mentioned, and replace or shim any framing members that are misaligned. The cut or factory ends of wallboard panels are not recessed to receive the tape and taping compound. · It should be obvious that the joist or stud on which you choose to locate the butt joint should be completely flat and in line with the framing on either

side, or preferably even a little "high" relative to its neighbors. This makes it possible to apply a layer of wallboard tape and covering compound without piling the butt joint higher with compound, so it makes an obvious ridge or bulge that will cast a shadow when it is sidelighted.

When planning wallboard layout, you should also plan the location of any header joints over or under windows or over doors. For walls that are less than 12 feet long, use full panels to span the entire length of the wall, and cut out the openings for the door or window. If the room is more than 12 feet long or wide and you must have a butt joint on the wall, plan the joint so it falls at midpoint (not at the corners) of the door or window header. Joints that occur at the corner of the opening will always crack, because the framing changes direction at this point (the header material is at right angles to the jack studs), so the wood framing members actually pull the joint apart as they shrink in opposite directions. Cut a notch in

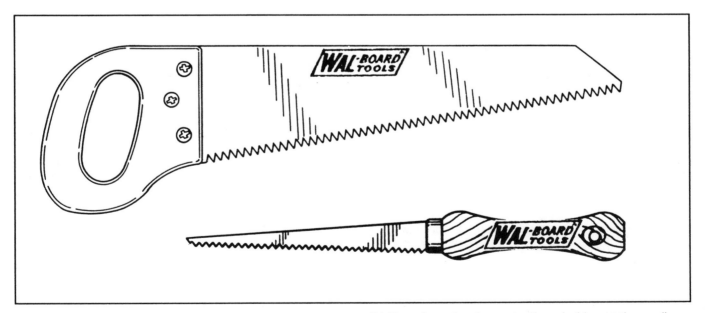

Wallboard saw has longer teeth and wider set than ordinary carpenter's saw, resists binding and dulling from plaster wallboard core. Wallboard utility saw has a straight handle that can be struck to drive saw tip through wallboard. Utility saw can be carried in tool pouch, used for making most wallboard cuts. Courtesy of Wal-Board Tools.

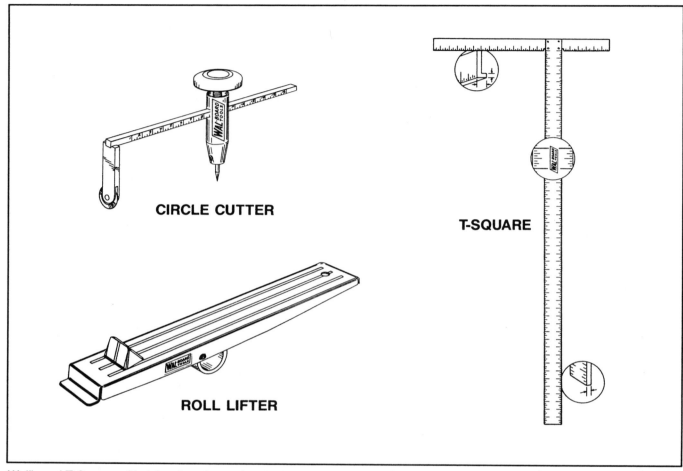

CIRCLE CUTTER

ROLL LIFTER

T-SQUARE

Wallboard T-Square with 4-foot long leg makes cutting wallboard easier, ensures straight cuts. Courtesy Wal-Board Tools.

Adjust the circle cutter so the distance from the pivot point to the cutter blade is equal to the radius of the hole to be cut. Place the pivot point of the circle cutter at the center of the hole

and turn the cutter wheel in a circle to mark the hole and cut through the face paper of the wallboard. Use a hammer to knock out the wallboard within the circle.

Wallboard lifter can be used to raise bottom course of wallboard up against top course on walls. Special lifters like these are low-cost, or you can use a prybar to lift the wallboard. Courtesy of Wal-Board Tools.

the wallboard so the joint occurs at or near the midpoint of the opening, not at the corners where it will crack, and where the finished joint may cause a slight bulge and make it difficult to trim the window and to match the miter joints.

WALLBOARD APPLICATION

If we could accomplish one thing with this book, it would be to settle the question: should you install wallboard so it is parallel to, or perpendicular to, the

framing? Many how-to texts recommend using 4-foot x 8-foot panels on the walls, installed parallel to the studs. This supposedly makes the wallboard easier to finish and eliminates the dreaded butt or end joint. But no manufacturer (for residential construction) recommends installing wallboard parallel to the framing rather than perpendicular to the framing.

On the subject of which direction to install wallboard, The Gypsum Wallboard Association says:

"In residential buildings with less than 8'1" ceiling heights it is preferred that wallboard be installed at right angles (perpendicular) to framing members; thus creating fewer joints to finish. On long walls, (wall)boards of maximum practical length (12-ft. unless access is limited) should be used to minimize the number of butt joints." ("Using Gypsum Board" page 7.)

United States Gypsum (USG) invented wallboard and named the product Sheetrock®. On the subject of which way to install wallboard, USG says: "Perpendicular application, recommended except in certain fire-rated partition construction or for predecorated panels, provides greater strength; reduces joint treatment and blocking needed (and) compensates for uneven framing alignment." (USG's "Systems Folder SA-924," page 1.)

Or listen to Gold Bond Building Products, a major manufacturer of wallboard and wallboard products: "Horizontal application (perpendicular, or with long edges at right angles to the framing) is preferred for it minimizes joints and strengthens the wall or ceiling." ("Gypsum Wallboard Products," p. 19.)

Why is it important to install gypsum wallboard panels perpendicular to the framing? Consider that this method:

1. Ties a maximum number of framing members together, for greater strength.

2. Uses wallboard in its strongest direction. Cut a piece of wallboard and try to break it across your knee while holding onto first the recessed or finished edges, then holding the two cut edges. You will see that wallboard is stronger across its width than along the length.

3. Installing wallboard perpendicular to the framing will reduce the footage of joints to be treated by at least 25 percent. Also, if you stand the panels up on the walls and install them

parallel to the studs, any joint that occurs on a twisted or warped stud will be very difficult to conceal.

4. Joint finishing is much easier for the workman when the joints are at waist (4 feet high) level, rather than parallel to the wall studs so the joints are 8 feet long, and spaced every 4 feet apart.

5. Joint banding, or a dark or shadowed appearance on treated wallboard joints, is a problem because of uneven suction or paint absorption on the wall or ceiling surface. It may show as dark streaks over joints on spray-textured ceilings or on painted walls. There are other problems that contribute to the degree of joint banding (we'll talk about these in Chapter 3, Finishing Wallboard), but joint placement is a definite contributor. On this subject USG states: "In the best installations, the gypsum panel (edge) joints run parallel with the direction of the light," or perpendicular to the framing on most residential walls and ceilings.

While the manufacturers and the Gypsum Wallboard Association and all its manufacturer/members have always recommended that wallboard installation be perpendicular to the framing, why the confusion (recommending parallel panel application) in how-to instructions? In a very few instances (see references to fire walls and prefinished wallboard in the USG quote above) parallel wallboard application is recommended. Too, in commercial or office construction where the ceilings are often suspended acoustical tiles and the walls are 8 feet high, carpenters often install ⅝-inch Firecode board, parallel to the steel studs. Seeing this, how-to writers may assume this is acceptable in residential construction. In any event, the quotes above should convince us all that perpendicular installation of wallboard panels is recommended throughout the industry as being superior for residential construction.

CHECKLIST FOR WALLBOARD INSTALLATION

• Always use the longest panels available. Twelve-foot long wallboard panels reduce the total footage of joints to be treated. Reducing the number and footage of wallboard joints means (1) less time and cost for finishing joints and (2) a reduction of the problems normally associated with joints, including joint cracking and joint banding.

• Buy wallboard of the right thickness for the job. Use $3/8$-inch thick wallboard only as a backer board under paneling, or in double layers for new construction or to match old plaster thickness in remodeling jobs. Use $1/2$-inch thick wallboard for single-layer coverage of framing up to 24 inches o.c. (on center). Use $5/8$-inch thick wallboard for fire or sound control (in double layers where needed). Also, use $5/8$-inch thick wallboard panels to cover ceilings with trusses set 24 inches o.c., or for ceilings that will support a heavy layer of thick insulation.

• Shipping damage is a common problem with the heavy but soft wallboard panels. Inspect wallboard panels for damage such as cracks or damaged corners or edges, and reject any panels that have been damaged.

• Don't try to install wallboard alone. Get a helper, one who is strong enough to handle the heavy lifting. If you can't find such a helper, hire the job done.

• Build sturdy scaffold, and custom-build it to match the height of the installers. Stooping or stretching while holding a load, common when the scaffold is not the right height, will quickly tire the workers.

• Always use wallboard screws, rather than nails, for wallboard installation.

• Always augment wallboard screws with wallboard or panel adhesives (except on walls/ceilings that have vapor barriers). The adhesives help eliminate minor problems with framing alignment and reduce the number of fasteners needed.

• Buy the proper wallboard installation tools, listed earlier in this chapter, to help make the job easier and the results more professional.

• Fit wallboard panels together loosely, without forcing them into place. Although wallboard has a low expansion rate, panels that are fitted tightly together may buckle from expansion.

• Be sure the studs at outside corners are straight and plumb, because any warped studs will result in a crooked corner. Cut the wallboard so it forms a 90-degree angle at the outside corners, because the wallboard should form a straight base to "seat" the metal corner bead. Set the corner bead on the corner so it is plumb and square, then nail the corner bead in place. Coat the corner beads with three coats of taping compound, allowing the compound to dry and shrink between each coat.

• Never use gypsum wallboard as a base for setting ceramic tile. Gypsum wallboard tends to absorb or "wick up" any moisture that penetrates behind the ceramic tile, and the soft plaster core will deteriorate from moisture contact, which eventually will lead to complete failure of the tile job. Use a cement/fiberglass panel such as USG's Durock as a substrate or base for mounting ceramic tile.

Durock by USG is a cement-based board that is used as a base for ceramic tile in any area where water may be a problem. Here, a workman nails Durock backer board in the bathtub area. Note that regular wallboard has been installed on the walls and ceilings of all but the tub area. Photo courtesy of USG.

Durock cement backer board can also be used as an underlayment on floors that will be tiled. Note the cement board can be either nailed or screwed in place, and can easily be cut using ordinary hand tools. Photo courtesy of USG.

3
Finishing Wallboard

It is impossible to do a perfect job of finishing wallboard if the wallboard is improperly installed. No amount of work or skill can overcome the problems a bad wallboard job presents. If butt or end joints are thoughtlessly positioned on warped or twisted framing, no number of trowel coats can overcome the problem and make the butt joints flat. If wallboard nails are used, pounded into the framing unevenly, the dimples or depressions over the nail heads will not be uniform, and the deeper dimples will require extra coats of compound to fill the dimples flat. Wallboard edges that are forced together may buckle or crack; wide gaps between wallboard joints are difficult to fill, and the compound may sag or crack. So the first requirement for getting a good wallboard job is to install the wallboard properly.

The goal of finishing wallboard is to apply wallboard tape and compound in a manner that will result in walls and ceilings that are attractive and blemish-free. Because most taping compounds contain about 50 percent water and harden as they give up moisture, there is a significant amount of shrinkage in the volume of the compound as this moisture is released. This shrinkage can be reduced by following the directions regarding the water/compound ratio closely when mixing dry powder compounds. If you will use ready-mixed all-purpose taping compounds, do not add too much water and over-thin the compound. Using compounds that are too thin will result in a sloppy job from material being too thin to handle, excessive shrinkage as the

compound dries, and edge-cracking along the edges of the wallboard tape.

The long or factory edges of wallboard panels are recessed to receive the tape and compound. If these edges were not recessed, the tape and compound would set upon the joints in a mound or curb shape, and would present objectionable ridges on the finished wall or ceiling. End or cut edges on wallboard obviously are not recessed, and this presents a problem for the wallboard finisher. If the stud or joist to which the butt joint is attached is "low," meaning the face of the framing member protrudes beyond the framing members on either side of the butt joint, this protrusion of the framing already means there is a ridge over the butt joint. If you now pile joint tape and compound over this ridge you will make it even more pronounced. That is why you should be sure the stud or joist at the butt joint is "high" compared to the neighboring framing. If the framing under the butt joint is "high," adding the joint tape and compound will fill the valley and make the butt joint flat, so it will be in plane with the surrounding area. Such a butt joint is easy to finish and to conceal.

Finishing instructions for wallboard recommend that all wallboard joints, dimples over screw or nail heads, and outside corner beads be treated with three coats, with a drying interval between coats to ensure full shrinkage of the compound. The shrinkage of each coat of compound as it dries or gives up moisture dictates that three coats are needed to overcome the shrinkage problem. For the inside

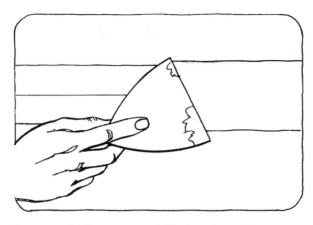

First coat of joint compound fills the channel formed by tapered edges of the wallboard.

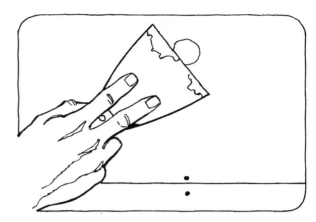

Spot nail heads with first coat of compound either as a separate operation before joint treatment or after applying tape.

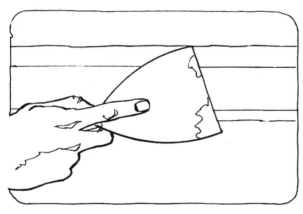

Embed tape directly over the joint. Tape full length of wall. Smooth joint compound around and over the tape to level the surface.

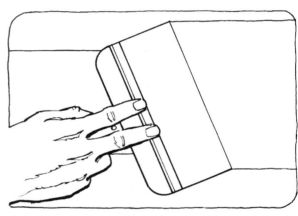

Second finishing coat is applied when the previous coat has dried. This coat is also spread thinly, feathering out 6 to 7 inches on each side of the joint. Finish nail spotting may be done at this time.

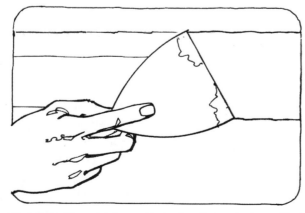

First finishing coat is applied after first coat has dried. Apply thinly and feather out 3 to 4 inches on each side of the joint.

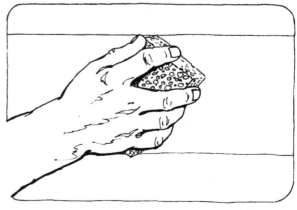

After twenty-four hours, smooth the finished joints with a damp sponge.

corners or angles, three coats are not needed: just apply the tape to the corners, let dry, then cover each side of the corner, alternating the side coated.

After three coats of compound have been applied it is difficult for the untrained eye to spot any possible problem areas. When the entire job has been given three coats of compound, it is best to check all treated surfaces at night, using a bare bulb to side-light the joints and screw heads to see if they look full and flat. Although three coats are standard treatment, extra coats may be needed if joints, nail-heads, or corners are not full and flat. This extra attention or "touch-up" phase is a very important part of the job procedure and should not be neglected.

TAPING WALLBOARD

For finishing wallboard, some tasks (such as covering or "spotting" screws or nails) require the use of broad knives. For finishing joints and outside corner beads you can choose either a plasterer's trowel or a wide taping knife. For the amateur the taping knife is a better tool choice than a trowel. To use a trowel you must carry the taping compound on a flat holder called a "hawk"; you can use a taping pan or an ordinary bread pan to hold the compound when finishing with a wide taping knife. The compound is much easier to handle when held in a taping pan. Although most tool stores offer corner taping knives, I have found that they are very difficult to use. Instead, use a 4-inch wide broad knife to smooth and cover inside corners.

Tools you will need for taping wallboard include 4-inch and 6-inch wide broad knives, 10-inch and 12-inch wide taping knives, a taping or "mud" pan to carry the compound, a measuring tape, hammer, nails and tin snips (for measuring, cutting, and nailing on corner beads), and a wallboard wet sander (preferred) or a sanding block and sandpaper.

You should also have a mixer of some sort to mix the wallboard compound. The best mixer is a wallboard mix bit chucked into a $1/2$-inch drill. Options include restaurant potato mixers (available in wall-

board tool supply houses) or even a clean, straight stick such as a 1 x 2. For cleaning up taping tools and plastic compound pails, buy a stiff bristle scrub brush.

Materials you will need include ready-mixed all-purpose taping compound in a 1- or 5-gallon plastic pail, all-steel corner beads as required, and wallboard tape.

Note that fiber (paper) wallboard tape is preferred over the self-sticking fiberglass tape for most d-i-y wallboard finishing applications. While fiberglass wallboard tape can be used for some repair jobs, it cannot be folded and applied to inside corners, and it works best when used with one of the fast-setting taping compounds if it is used for taping wallboard joints.

There are no set rules for procedure when taping and finishing wallboard, but professional applicators generally divide the job into three coats: taping, second coat (first trowel coat), and third or finish trowel coat. These coats are divided into working with joints, inside corners, outside corners, and screw or nail heads. Follow this orderly procedure:

Before beginning the taping and finishing, be sure you have permanent heating so you can hold the work area temperature at a constant level. Do not use temporary space heaters to heat the work space during cold weather. Letting temperatures fluctuate during the finishing or decorating period can contribute to a variety of failures and problems in the finished job. These potential problems include rusting over the screw or nail heads, from too-slow drying; expansion and contraction of the wallboard panels, which cause ridging or deformation of the tape over the joints: delayed shrinkage of the taping compound, which can occur after decorating when permanent heat is introduced into the work space; and discoloration of the finish paint coat due to residual moisture in the compound. In cold weather, do not undertake the taping and finishing phases until you have installed a permanent heat source. Then set the thermostat at a comfortable working level and leave it alone, keeping the temperature constant in the work area during the period when finishing and painting are being done.

During the first or taping coat all corner beads should be nailed on (this may also be done as the last step of installing wallboard). Then joints or seams are taped first, because the ends of the joint tape should be concealed by the inside corner tape. When all joints and inside corners have been reinforced with tape, a fill coat should be applied over all nail or screw heads, and over outside corner beads. It is also advisable to "backfill" or spread a very thin coat of compound over the taped joints at this time. All this taping and preliminary filling is considered to be part of the taping or first coat.

A prime concern when taping wallboard is to work on small areas at a time so the taping compound does not "crust" or surface-dry and cause blisters (loose spots) in the tape. Keep temperatures in the 60-70 degree range, both to retard drying of the compound and for worker comfort. If necessary to retard drying of the compound while performing the taping, set a humidifier in the work area to keep humidity levels up (only while the actual work is being done).

To apply compound to joints, start with any butt or end joints, or joints in headers over and under windows or over doors. Use the 6-inch broad knife to apply the compound over the joint. Then embed the fiber tape in the wet compound, so the tape is centered over the crack of the joint. Then use the 6-inch knife to wipe away any excess compound under and alongside the tape. When butt and header joints are taped, tape the long, recessed joints.

When all joints are taped, begin taping the corners. Use a 4-inch broad knife to apply compound to both sides of the inside corners. Then fold the tape in the middle. If you look closely at the fiber tape you will see a small ridge at the center. Fold the tape at the ridge, holding the end of the tape pinched between your thumb and forefinger, with your small finger curled around the tape to keep it centered and to

guide it between the thumb and forefinger. Now pull the tape slowly through the fingers with the free hand. Careful here: If you pull the paper too quickly or it becomes off-center you can get a nasty paper cut from the tape.

Now position the folded tape squarely into the corner and use the 4-inch broad knife to embed the tape and to remove any excess compound. Be careful to form the corner tape into square, 90-degree corners. Corners that are not square, or are rounded by misaligned tape or by compound buildup, will make the placement of baseboard and other trim very difficult.

With all tape in place, use the 10-inch wide taping knife to fill all metal corner beads. Extend the compound coat out the full width of the taping knife, leaving the exact corner of the metal bead, called the *screed*, bare — do not cover the point of the corner bead with taping compound. Also use the 6-inch broad knife to coat or spot the screw heads. For spotting the screw heads, dab a walnut-sized ball of compound over the screw head, then, holding the knife at right angles to the surface, wipe the extra compound from the face of the wallboard, leaving only the dimple over the screw head filled.

Note that no edges, trowel marks, or spilled wallboard compound should be left on the wall or ceiling. Wallboard compound becomes very hard when it dries, and sanding is a dirty and difficult job. Use the taping knives to wipe away all excess compound while it is still wet and easy to remove. Also, use a taping knife or a floor scraper to pick up any compound spilled on the floor, while the compound is still soft and easy to remove.

Again using the 6-inch broad knife, wipe a very thin covering coat over all taped joints. This coat should span the width of the recessed joint and fill the cavity. With all surfaces covered, this completes the first or taping coat.

After completing the first (taping) coat, or any time you will be away from the project for a time, use a fiber scrub brush to clean down the compound on

outside corners

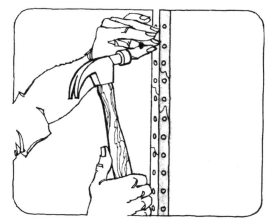

Outside corners are reinforced with corner bead. Bead is secured by nailing through the wallboard to framing underneath.

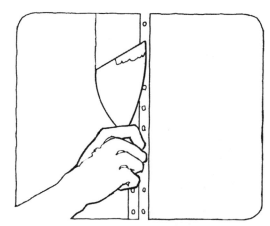

Joint compound is applied with a broad knife over the corner bead flange. First coat should be approximately 6 inches wide, second coat about 9 inches wide, on each side of corner.

inside corners

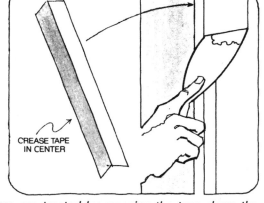

CREASE TAPE IN CENTER

Inside corners are treated by creasing the tape down the center before adhering it to the joint compound.

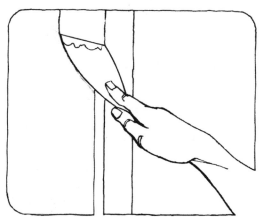

Corner is then treated with one coat in two steps. Treat one side and let dry; then treat other side.

For curved edges, use special arch corner bead, snipping one flange to the center at approximately 1-inch intervals. Bend to conform to the curve and nail uncut side through the wallboard

into framing. Flatten cut tabs against the wall and nail similarly.
Illustrations courtesy of Gold Bond.

Use a taper's mud pan to carry taping compound to the job. Wire tape holder on belt, either bought or shaped from a coat hanger, frees up hands while keeping tape easy to reach. Photo courtesy of Gold Bond.

Apply wallboard compound over the center of the joint, then align the wallboard tape and wipe the excess compound from under the tape. Photo courtesy of USG.

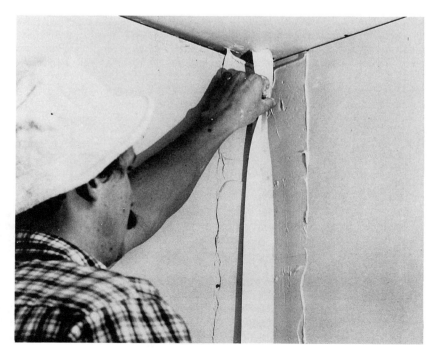

the sides of the plastic pail. Cover the taping compound with water and press the replaceable lid on the pail. The taping compound will last for weeks without drying out if kept covered. To begin using the compound again, pour off the covering water and stir the compound to mix in any remaining surface moisture.

Let the compound on the first or taping coat dry completely. Usually this complete drying means waiting overnight, but low temperature or high humidity in the workplace may delay drying. Because the compound fill is deepest over the metal corner bead, these corners will dry slowest. When the compound appears dry, test the compound on the corner bead with your fingernail, or with the tip of a broad knife, to see if the compound has hardened. If the compound seems hard, it is dry enough to recoat. Note that the surface of the compound will dry first, so a visual inspection alone is not proof that the compound is dry. Test compound for hardness before proceeding with the next coat.

Use the 10-inch taping knife to apply a second or leveling coat of compound to all joints and outside corner beads. First, coat the butt or end joints. Keep in mind that the goal is to use the compound fill to make all joints level: do not pile the compound high or create a crown over the joints.

When the butt or end joints are covered with a second coat of compound, coat all long or recessed joints. Again, the goal is to fill the recess in the joint so it is flat. Do not pile excess compound over the joint. When all joints are covered, use the taping knife to coat all corner beads with a second coat of compound.

When the joints are dry use the 4-inch broad knife to smooth one side of the inside corners. If you have applied the corner tape properly, being sure all corners are square, the corner finishing is merely a matter of covering the edges of the corner tape. Cover only one side of the corner tape, and let that side dry. You will cover the opposite side of the corner tape when you apply the third and final coat.

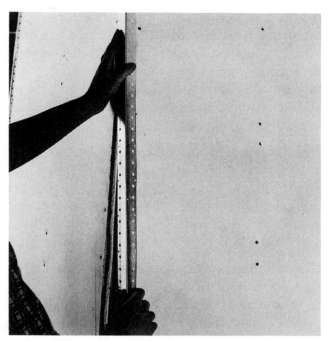

Center metal corner beads on outside corners, and use wallboard nails to secure them in place. Drive nails in every second nail hole and avoid toenailing, so corner beads will not be pulled to either side. Photo courtesy of USG.

Outside corner beads have a high point or screed. Use the screed as a guide for filling beads with knife or trowel. Apply three coats to corner beads, allowing taping compound to dry between coats. Photo courtesy of USG.

Use the 6-inch broad knife to apply a second coat of compound over all screw heads. Do not pile compound in a mound over the screw: fill the dimple in the wallboard and wipe away all excess compound from the area around the screw head. You do not want a series of bumps on the wall, so keep the material flat.

This completes the second coat. Again, it is important that you let this fill or leveling coat dry completely, so it will shrink where it will before you apply the final coat of compound. After the compound has dried, use a broad knife or sander to remove any blobs or "slag" from the wallboard.

The third coat is done following the same procedure used on the second coat. Use the 12-inch taping knife to coat all butt joints, recessed joints, and outside corner beads. The point of using a wider taping knife on each succeeding coat is to ensure that you cover the edges of the previous coats, leaving a smoother job and reducing any need for sanding. After coating the joints and corner bead use the 4-inch broad knife to coat the opposite side of all inside corners. Be careful at this point that you do not pile compound deep over the apex or point of the inside corner. Excess compound at the apex of the corner will cause material cracks, or cracks in the compound only, to appear at corners.

Give the screw heads a final covering coat, using the 6-inch broad knife and wiping all surface compound away. This completes the traditional three-coat finishing job on wallboard. As suggested earlier in the chapter, wait until the compound is completely dry, then bring a trouble light and bare light bulb into the work area. Hold the bare light bulb against each ceiling and wall in turn, and visually inspect each surface for hollow joints or other blemishes. Touch up as needed, recoating each defect to eliminate any problems.

One common lament of do-it-yourselfers is that sanding wallboard is hard and dirty work. We advise you to use a wallboard wet sander to smooth the wallboard compound, rather than using sandpa-per. The wallboard wet sander is a sponge covered with an abrasive nylon covering or screen. The trick to using a wet sander is to smooth the compound as you go. Don't wait until the job is completely dry, as you do with sandpaper, to smooth the material. Rather, keep a pail of clean water and the wet sander at hand as you do the wallboard finish work. As soon as the compound appears to be firm (but not completely dry) dip the wet sander in the water pail and smooth the compound. The compound will readily soften if you work it before it becomes completely hardened.

One drawback to decorating wallboard is that the conventional taping procedure leaves taping compound over the screw heads, inside and outside corners, and joints, while the balance of the face paper on the wallboard is left untreated. This means that in reality you are trying to paint two different materials: the compound on the treated area, and the paper face on the untreated wallboard. The problem is that the two materials will accept and absorb paint unequally, and will yield a finish paint coat that is uneven in texture and sheen. The difference in the two material surfaces is accentuated by any sanding, where rough sandpaper scuffs or "raises the nap" of the face paper on the wallboard. This means that treated wallboard areas will "shadow" or stand out against the field or untreated area of the wallboard.

To eliminate this problem, the wallboard manufacturers recommend that, after completing the three-coat finishing process, you cover the entire surface of the wallboard with a thin or skim coat of taping compound. Obviously, covering all the paper face of the wallboard with compound will result in a surface that is uniform in porosity or suction, eliminating the checkerboard effect of having to paint alternate areas of paper and compound. Note: This skim or covering coat of compound is not intended to be done in lieu of the third finishing coat. You must complete the traditional three-coat finish process, let the final coat dry, and then cover all surfaces with a thin coating of compound.

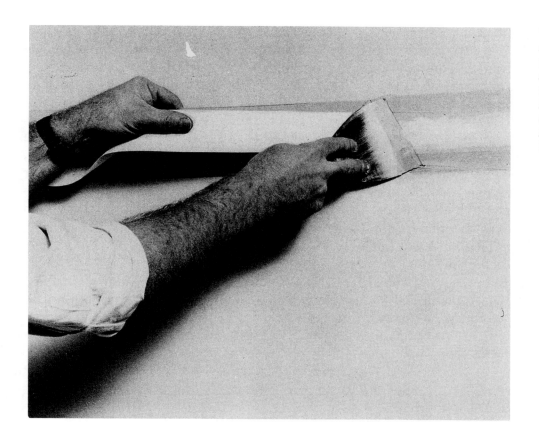

To tape inside corners, fold tape along center crease, apply wallboard compound to each side of the corner, then position and smooth corner tape. Let dry and apply one light covering coat on each side of the folded tape. Photo courtesy of USG.

Use a wallboard pole sander or a wet sander to sand and smooth wallboard compound. Pole sanders have a universal joint at the sander head, so you can use them on either walls or ceilings, at any angle. Photo courtesy of USG.

Skim coating the entire surface takes a considerable amount of time, and can be a messy process. It requires some skill with the trowel or taping knife to apply the skim coat and to get a smooth job. If you decide to do this yourself, one tip is to use a humidifier in the space to keep humidity levels up and thus to slow compound drying. Another tip is to thin the compound so that it can be troweled onto the wall and immediately be sheared away, leaving only a wet coat. Or, working with a partner, thin the wallboard compound with water to a consistency thin enough that the compound can be applied to the wallboard using a paint roller. The technique is for one person to roll a coat of compound onto the wallboard, while the partner follows along, using the taping knife to wipe the coat smooth and to remove excess compound. As the material becomes firm, but before it is completely dry, use ordinary sponges, wetted frequently, to wipe the compound smooth.

Another technique, using the taping knife only, can be done by a single worker. The difficult part of the job is trying to cover the wallboard without leaving trowel marks in the finish. Instead of trying to cover the entire surface at one time, make a series of horizontal covering coats, spaced about 10 inches apart, and let them dry. Then, when these strips are dry, trowel compound over the bare strips between, making the coating of compound continuous over the entire surface. Using this technique will eliminate the numerous trowel marks or ridges that often result when one tries to "plaster" or thin coat the wallboard in one application.

A couple of precautions are in order. Textured ceilings, often sprayed-on, are the norm for wallboard construction. And in recent years, various styles of wall textures have become popular, especially in southern or western houses where the Spanish/Mexican influence is strong. Because of

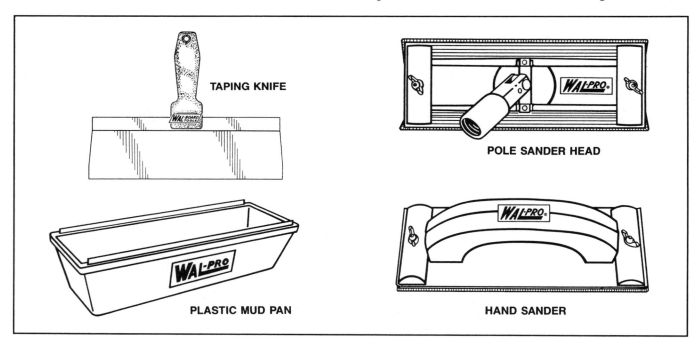

TAPING KNIFE

POLE SANDER HEAD

PLASTIC MUD PAN

HAND SANDER

Plastic mud pan is lightweight, has steel edges for wiping tools clean. Use the mud pan to carry taping compound. Pan can be used with finishing knives up to 12 inches wide. Courtesy of Wal-Board Tools.

Wallboard sanders include a universal head that can be attached to a pole for sanding either ceilings or walls, and a hand sander. Sponge with a vinyl scrub cover can also be used to wet sand wallboard and avoid sanding dust. Courtesy Wal-Board Tools.

the rough and irregular surface of texture and texture paints, many manufacturers advertise their products as cure-alls for covering rough walls. While texture paints may cover minor variations in suction or absorption and thus eliminate the need for skim-coating the entire surface, no texture or texture paint product can make a wall level or fill hollow joints or the dimples over screw heads. Texture painting will not eliminate the need to use tape to reinforce the joints and inside corners, nor will it substitute for finishing coats of compound. You should always complete the three-coat wallboard finishing process to be sure all surfaces and joints are flat and smooth. The texturing process should be done only to achieve some desired pattern effect, and should not be viewed as a cover-up or substitution for the wallboard finishing process.

A final warning: Alkyd or oil-base primer is recommended for use on wallboard *only* on ceilings that will be spray textured. Wallboard manufacturers have *never* recommended oil-base primers or sealers as a first coat over bare wallboard. Oil primers are slow drying and will raise the nap on the wallboard face paper, thus leaving a wallboard surface that appears smooth over the areas that have been treated with compound, and rough over any areas where the oil covers bare paper. Instead, use a full-bodied interior latex paint as a first coat over wallboard, then use any alkyd/oil or latex topcoat as a finish. In fact, United States Gypsum recommends using a latex paint as a first coat, even when the ceilings or walls will be spray textured. USG's choice for a first coat over wallboard, *regardless* of whether you will finish with paint, wall covering, or texture, is their own special latex wallboard primer, called First Coat. First Coat has enough solids to help conceal any differences in surface texture, thus acting as a fine *primer*, while also acting as a *sealer* to prevent uneven paint absorption, which may result in uneven sheen. Who knows more about wallboard than USG? Nobody does: take their word for it and use First Coat, or a quality full-bodied latex paint, as a base coat over wallboard.

4

Patching Walls and Ceilings

Most repairs on walls and ceilings can be done by the homeowner. Problems on walls or ceilings may be due to aging of the plaster or wallboard, to water damage from leaking plumbing or from a leaking roof, to impact damage from Junior's tricycle or from a doorknob hitting a wall, or to cracking caused by a variety of factors. To make successful repairs, one should understand and correct the source of the problem. For example, wall or ceiling repairs for water damage should not be done until the source of the water penetration — leaking roof or leaking piping — has been found and repaired.

Many wall and ceiling problems can be solved by using a common repair approach, whether the wall/ceiling construction is plaster or wallboard. For example, repair of small holes due to impact damage is the same for wallboard or for plaster construction. Most cracks are structural, meaning they are caused by expansion or contraction of the structure (framing), whether they occur in plaster or in wallboard (more about this later). A few repair problems, however, are peculiar to either plaster or wallboard alone, and we will discuss these unique problems first.

PLASTER

Plaster construction is a system in which a base of lath is first applied over the framing. The base may be either wood, rock, or gypsum lath or steel (wire) lath. Over this lath base two coats of plaster are applied. The first coat, also called the brown coat because of its brown or gray color, is troweled over the lath. The brown coat can be spread over the area with a straightedge called a darby. The brown coat thus provides the means of leveling and building bulk or mass into the wall/ceiling. The bulk or mass of the construction determines characteristics of the wall/ceiling, such as the fireproofing and sound-proofing values.

When the first or brown coat is set or hardened, a second coat — a white or lime coat — is applied. This white or lime coat is thinner than the brown coat, can be troweled extremely smooth, and provides a hard, protective coat that readily accepts any decorative treatment, such as paint or wall covering.

The point in reviewing plaster construction is to note that because plaster is a three-stage construction, there is a bond between each layer of plaster — brown coat to lath, lime coat to brown coat — and a bond failure may occur between any two stages of the plaster. This may be due to poor workmanship in building the wall/ceiling system but is most often due either to aging of the material or to impact or water damage that destroys the bond between any two of the three layers.

In plaster with wood lath construction there is no adhesive bond between the brown coat and the wood. The brown coat sticks in place because of a

Ready-mix patcher such as 222 Lite Spackling Paste can be used for patching most small blemishes in wallboard, concrete, or plaster. Product offers low shrinkage with little sanding necessary. Photo courtesy of UGL.

Modern repair products make obsolete old patching techniques. The Plaster Wall Patch shown offers mixing ease plus low shrinkage for patching voids in plaster. Photo courtesy of USG.

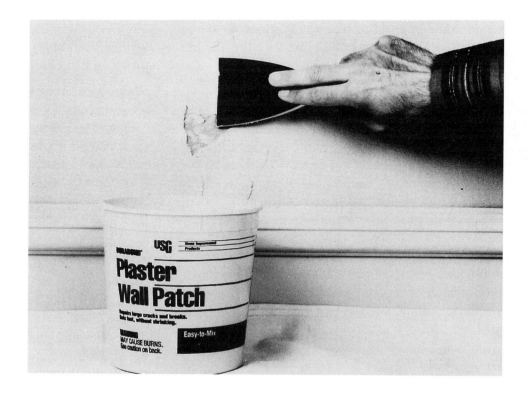

mechanical bond caused by plaster that is forced between the 1/4-inch wide cracks between the laths. This plaster slumps or curls behind the wood lath and locks the plaster in place. These plaster curls are called "keys." As age and vibration affect these keys, they break off, leaving the plaster face coat with no means of support. When key loss area is limited, a portion of the face plaster releases, and there may be a hole in the plaster. In this case the loose plaster area is removed and a new coat(s) of patching plaster is troweled in place.

One way to check the condition of the plaster is to press against the plaster with the palm of your hand. Press hard and be alert to any "give" or movement of the plaster. If the plaster feels spongy or loose, you will know that there is a bond failure, and you should attempt to correct it (see below) before the bond failure becomes total over the entire wall/ ceiling.

You can often actually see an area of loose plaster because it is bulged from the lath. If the plaster face is loose but has not yet collapsed, you may be able to reattach the plaster to the lath. This must be done by professionals who inject an adhesive between the lath and plaster layers and thus bond the two together again (see Chapter 1). There are also large-headed screws that can be used to screw the loose plaster to the wood lath. These screws can be purchased at any outlet that sells plaster and concrete products and supplies.

If the key loss area is widespread, *all* the face plaster will collapse and release from the lath. Then the old plaster must be totally removed and the wall/ceiling must be completely replastered. Doing a total replastering job is beyond the ability of most do-it-yourselfers, so it should be done by a professional.

An inter-coat plaster failure that occurs over a limited area can be successfully repaired by the homeowner. The problems one encounters in plaster patching include a failure of the patching plaster to bond or stick to the lath or to the remaining base coat; a failure of the patching plaster to stick to the edges of the existing plaster surrounding the damaged portion; and premature drying of the patching plaster, which may result in cracks between the existing plaster and the new patching material.

To prevent premature drying and cracking of the patch, the old approach was to wet the remaining plaster and base lath with water from a wet paint brush. In most cases this does not solve the problem, because the applicator fails to wet the old plaster completely. Because the lath and plaster are very dry they must be wetted repeatedly, to the point of complete saturation. If the repair surfaces are only superficially wetted, premature drying will still occur, and the patching plaster will crack and show excessive shrinkage.

Rather than wetting the base lath and existing plaster with water, use a latex bonding adhesive. These bonding adhesives look like white latex paint and are sold to improve the bond for patches on damaged concrete or plaster. An example of this product would be Quikrete Concrete Bonding Adhesive. Ask your dealer to suggest his own brand of product.

One precautionary suggestion: I have seen many texts in which plaster patching instructions showed a piece of metal (wire) lath being inserted into the plaster hole, *atop intact wood lath*. This is unnecessary. If there is no lath remaining in the plaster hole, cut wire lath to size and insert the wire lath in the hole to replace the missing wood lath. This is necessary to provide support for the plaster until the plaster dries. But if there is lath remaining at the bottom of the hole, it is unnecessary and a waste of time to insert wire lath also. The lath merely supports the wet plaster — you don't need two layers of lath. Just let the wood lath provide the support, and use a paint brush to coat the lath and the edges of the existing plaster.

An old pro's trick, used long before they invented latex bonding adhesive, was to coat the old lath and plaster with varnish. Then, while the varnish was still wet, we troweled in the patching plaster over the still-wet varnish. The patching plaster created heat as it began to harden, and the combination of the heat plus the sticky varnish "welded" the new patching plaster in place.

WALLBOARD

If properly installed, wallboard construction is less prone to cracking than is plaster. Plaster, being brittle, will crack if there is any stress from expansion or contraction. Wallboard, being attached with fasteners (screws or nails), will yield or give slightly and will resist cracking. But, being attached with fasteners, wallboard is prone to fastener (nail or screw) "pops."

Nail or fastener pops were once believed to be caused by the fasteners becoming loose. In fact, the problem is due to (1) using too-long fasteners and (2) the shrinkage or "settling" of the framing members. What happens, according to studies done on the subject by United States Gypsum, is that the framing actually shrinks away from the wallboard and the head of the fastener protrudes, leaving a "pop" on the head. Because the pop is caused by shrinking lumber, the *severity* of the pop will be directly proportional to the length of the fastener. In other words, a screw or nail that penetrates one-half the thickness of the stud or joist will pop relative to the thickness loss of 1/2 the framing. In contrast, a fastener that has sufficient holding power, but is so short that it penetrates only 1/2 to 3/4 inch of the wood will experience a pop at the head that is equal to the shrinkage of only the 1/2 inch of wood. The shrinkage in so little wood is negligible, so the pop will be nonexistent or at least superficial.

Now, we have known of this relationship for years: the degree of pop on the head of the fastener is directly proportional to the depth to which the fastener penetrates the wood framing. So to prevent fastener pops it is very important that you use fasteners that are long enough to provide sufficient holding power but no longer. When using wallboard screws to attach 1/2-inch thick wallboard, use

screws that are 1 inch long. These screws will provide plenty of holding power to secure the wallboard without unnecessary depth penetration of the framing member. If you are nailing on wallboard, use 1 1/4-inch long ring-shank wallboard nails. Yes, you can buy longer wallboard nails: but they are intended for use on 5/8-inch thick wallboard. Don't overlook this important point. Wallboard manufacturers developed ring-shank nails and wallboard screws so they could get maximum holding power while limiting the fastener's penetration into the wood.

Keep in mind that the worst fastener popping will take place as the house settles, during the first year after it is built. After the house is occupied, and heated and cooled for one year, the moisture level of the framing will stabilize with only minor future changes in lumber moisture content. (These minor changes are enough to cause structural cracks, however.)

The point is that you should ignore any popped fasteners you see for at least one year before you undertake repair. After one year, or when you are ready to redecorate, press with the flat of your hand on the wallboard and drive a wallboard screw alongside any popped fastener, into the framing beneath, pulling the wallboard back into contact with the framing. Then use a hammer to drive any popped fastener head below the surface of the wallboard. Give all the new and re-driven fasteners three coats of wallboard compound, letting each coat dry before recoating. Smooth the repairs with a wallboard wet sander or sponge and give the entire wall or ceiling two coats of latex paint. When you have repaired all popped fasteners, you will have eliminated the problem forever. If you have followed the preceding directions carefully, the fastener pops will not recur.

PATCHING HOLES

There are two major causes of patching failures: using the wrong material and using the wrong tools.

For very deep fills on holes, such as plaster that is gone down to the lath, use patching plaster rather than wallboard compound to make the repair. Patching plaster does not shrink as much as wallboard compound, so patching plaster should be used to make hole repairs on deep fills.

If the holes are less than 4 inches in diameter, don't bother to fill them. Instead, use one of the peel-and-stick patches found in paint departments. These patches have a metallic foil center and are covered with fiberglass mesh that is treated with an adhesive. Just peel off the backer and apply the patch over any hole, in wallboard or in plaster. Then cover the patch with two coats of wallboard compound, allowing drying time between the two coats. Smooth with a wet sander and prime or paint.

One point about the peel-and-stick patches: one customer, standing near me at a paint counter, mumbled something negative when he saw me pick up this type of patch. His protest as I understood it was that I was somehow "cheating" or making an unsatisfactory repair. A wall (or ceiling) in a house is basically a privacy screen between two areas. Some walls must have certain qualities, such as fireproofing or soundproofing, but most are just a curtain to separate two areas. You do not change any meaningful characteristics of a wall or ceiling by repairing them with the peel-and-stick patches. As a matter of fact, these patches eliminate the problem of bond failures between the lath and plaster or between the patching plaster and the existing plaster. They also solve the problem of having no framing to anchor a patch to when repairing wallboard. Using such patches will not alter the values of the wall in any significant way, and it is not "better" or "right" to use the old, tedious plaster-patching techniques. Using the easy patches is simply a much better way to achieve the patch, and it is ridiculous to make a patch in any other way if these handy patches will do. Just measure the diameter of the hole to be patched and be sure to buy a patch large enough to span the hole. Patches are available up to 6 inches in diameter.

If the hole is in wallboard and it is too big to be covered with the peel-and-stick patches, you must cut out the damaged section of the wallboard. Cut back to the studs or joists on either side of the damaged area, and use a sharp razor knife to cut away the wallboard back to the center of each framing member. Then cut a piece of wallboard to fit the hole, and nail the patch piece in place, fastening the wallboard to the framing on either side of the hole. Tape and patch the repair area with three coats, following the directions given in Chapter 3, Finishing Wallboard.

Remember, too, to use the right tool for the job. When you are patching a hole, use a knife or trowel that is wider than the hole being patched. If you use a narrow patching tool that does not span the entire hole, you will end up with a cavity that is not full and a patch that has a series of ridges or trowel marks. Using a wide tool enables you to finish the patching material with a minimum of repeat strokes and will result in a much smoother patch with less sanding required.

PATCHING CRACKS

Many how-to texts make a distinction between *structural* cracks and *hairline* cracks. To a tradesman, a hairline crack is usually a minor surface crack in the material — plaster or wallboard compound — and is generally short. By contrast, a structural crack is one that is caused by movement of the house framing or structure (hence the name "structural") and occurs where framing or structure is joined at opposing angles to each other. For example, the jack and king studs at both sides of a window or door opening are set at right angles to the studs in the headers, so when the two pieces shrink they shrink in opposite directions; i.e., they shrink apart, pulling the covering material of plaster or wallboard in opposing directions. This opposing stress obviously causes cracks in the wall or ceiling material.

Many people are disappointed when cracks that have been filled with plaster or spackle reopen within months, marring a new paint job. The fact is that framing lumber, when placed in a house, contains about 19 percent moisture: an 8-foot long 2 x 4 stud contains about a cup of water. Note that these figures refer to lumber that is *kiln dried*: green lumber has an even higher moisture content.

As the house is assembled, even more moisture is introduced into the interior. Concrete floors and walls in basements; plaster, wallboard compound, and paint all contain water and add to the interior moisture levels of the house. All this moisture affects the framing or structure of the house.

When the house is finished, the occupants will try to control interior temperature and moisture levels. We do this by heating, cooling, and humidifying the air in the house. During the first year, the house framing lumber will give up moisture, and framing lumber will shrink. This moisture loss and shrinkage is called *settling*, and many structural cracks and screw or nail pops occur during this settling period.

After the house is occupied for a full year, the moisture content of the framing lumber becomes relatively stable, at between 8 and 12 percent. Most cracking and fastener pops have occurred, and the interior of the house will suffer little movement as long as it is occupied. The bad news is that there will always be slight movement of the house structure, as humidity and temperature levels fluctuate with the seasons. It is this slight expansion/contraction that causes patched cracks to reopen periodically and to defeat your attempts to get a permanent patch. This is why we always advise you to reinforce any crack when you patch it.

If ceiling joists are too small, you will often see a plaster crack that runs the full length of a room, at or very near the center of the room. These center cracks are parallel to the long walls or length of the room, and occur when the ceiling joists sag or deflect under the weight of the ceiling plaster and the ceiling insulation. If the joists deflect to an excessive degree, the brittle plaster will crack. Because the point of maximum joist deflection is at the center of the joist, that is where the crack in plaster will occur.

Other locations where structural cracks commonly occur are at the corners of headers, over and under windows and over doors; at corners where two walls meet, especially at the outside corners of the house where two exterior walls meet; at corners where ceilings meet walls; and at any point, such as in stairways, where two floors meet and wallboard joints occur where floor joists meet studs and floor sheathing lumber. Any place where one piece of lumber meets another piece of lumber is a poor location for a joint. That is why the wallboard industry warns us not to make joints in wallboard at header corners above windows or doors.

The purpose of trying to recognize the cause of a crack is that structural cracks must be reinforced if you intend to make a permanent repair. If a brittle patching material such as patching plaster or spackle-type patcher is used to patch a structural crack, that crack will simply reopen the next time the structure moves. For our purposes, the best approach is to treat every crack as though it were structural (as most are) and reinforce the crack to attempt a permanent repair.

Whether a crack occurs in plaster or wallboard, and regardless of whether you believe it to be a structural crack, always follow this procedure when patching cracks.

The first step for patches on plaster cracks is to press on the wall/ceiling along each side of the crack to see if the plaster is loose from the lath. If the plaster is loose over a wide area, you may have to remove the plaster to make a permanent repair; i.e., remove the loose plaster and fill the hole with patching plaster.

If the plaster along the crack is not loose, or the crack is in wallboard, use a broad knife to clean all loose material from the crack. Then prefill the crack with premixed wallboard taping compound and allow it to dry, usually within a few hours or overnight.

Fast-N-Final Spackling is premixed and dries without sagging or shrinking. Light-weight, fast-drying patch products help you patch and paint in one day. Photo courtesy of USG.

Peel-and-stick fiberglass patches, available in sizes up to six inches, provide a modern solution to patching holes in wallboard or plaster. No backing is needed: just peel the patch and stick it to the wall or ceiling. Photo by the author.

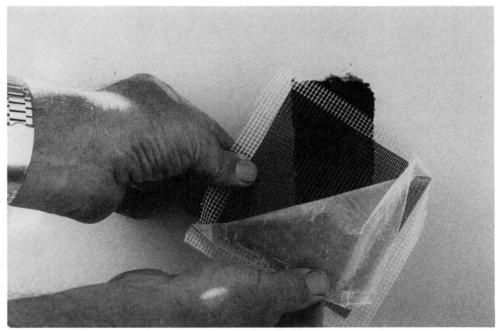

Strong wire mesh patch, with fiberglass adhesive backing, yields both repair ease and patch strength to repair area. Photo by the author.

Adhesive patches can be covered with spackle or with wallboard compound. Photo by the author.

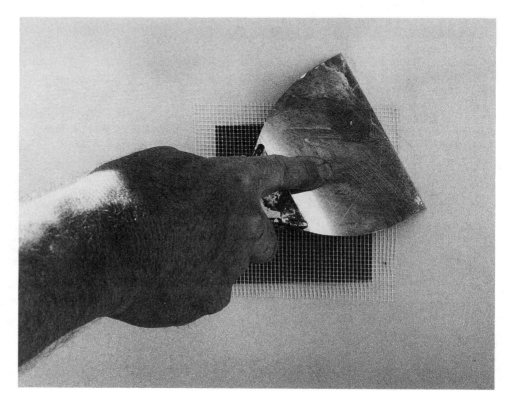

When the prefilled crack is dry, use a sanding block to sand away any ridge at the joint. Then use a 6-inch wide broad knife to "butter" the crack, spreading wallboard compound over the crack in the same way you would do to tape a joint in wallboard. Note that most cracks occur in a wandering or crooked shape, not in a straight line. Using paper (fiber) wallboard tape, center the tape over the crack and press the tape into the wet compound. If the crack changes direction, do not wrinkle the tape to turn it. Instead, cut the wallboard tape at the turn and start off in the new direction.

Don't try to tape too much at one time. You should apply taping compound only to a short crack, or a portion of a long crack, at one time. This lets you be sure that the wallboard compound is still wet, so the tape will adhere to the crack. Trying to spread too much compound at one time will result in surface crusting or drying of the compound, and will yield loose spots or "blisters" in the wallboard tape.

When the tape is in place, use the 6-inch broad knife to wipe away any excess wallboard compound. Leave only a thin film of compound under the wallboard tape, and wipe the edges of the tape smooth. Immediately put a thin or skim coat of compound over the tape to help conceal the tape edges. Wipe it clean and let the tape dry before proceeding.

When the tape is dry, use the broad knife or taping knife to apply a *very thin* layer of wallboard compound over the tape. Be aware that if you pile the compound high you will have future material cracks — cracks in the surface of the patching material itself — the next time the structure moves. Avoid any compound buildup over the crack.

When the first covering coat of compound is dry, often within hours (remember, it's *thin*), apply another covering coat. The purpose of these two coats is to level and conceal the reinforcing wallboard tape so its outline will not show through the finish coat and paint.

When the patching over the crack(s) is dry, smooth it with your wallboard wet sander. Then apply two coats of latex paint over the entire surface.

Most structural cracks that have been reinforced with paper wallboard tape and compound will not recur. In a few instances, the wall or ceiling will be subject to exaggerated movement when humidity levels and temperatures change, and no amount of reinforcement will prevent cracks from reopening. In these cases there is no remedy except to "chase the cracks" — to patch the crack anew each time it opens again. But the vast majority of cracks will stay patched if you follow the procedure given above.

If a wall or ceiling is covered with a network of fine cracks, occurring randomly over the entire area, consider having a painter hang canvas or underliner (sometimes called "blank stock" because it has no color or pattern) over the walls or ceilings affected. When this underliner is in place you can then paint or paper as your own tastes dictate, with assurance that your decorating job will not be spoiled by these cracks. Be sure to ask the decorator if your particular walls or ceilings will accept this treatment successfully; some may not, because there may be advanced deterioration of the plaster or paint.

In one case I encountered as a pro, a young couple had run an inhalator or a steamer for a prolonged period while trying to help their child overcome a bad case of bronchitis. They had closed off the child's room and raised the humidity levels in the room for a prolonged period. When they removed the steamer, the paint coat was covered with "alligatored" paint — paint that had hundreds of small random cracks. I was asked to remove this condition, or to remove the many coats of old paint.

I attempted to remove the old paint, using a body grinder such as those used in auto body shops. I soon gave up on this approach as being very dirty and very ineffective. Finally, using a pad sander, I lightly sanded the entire surface of the four walls (the ceilings had not been affected). Then, with wallboard compound I had thinned to the consistency of heavy cream, I applied a thin or skim coat over the entire surface of the four walls. When this dried I applied a second skim coat, then sanded the entire surface. The couple repainted without seeing any further cracking, and several years later the cure was still effective.

Skim coating, or troweling a thin coat of compound over all the wall or ceiling surfaces in a room (or an entire house, on new wallboard), can ensure a smooth, new surface when applied to new wallboard or on problem walls or ceilings. It is difficult for the amateur to trowel an entire surface in this manner, and you may choose to leave skim coating up to a professional. However, in my decorating days I used the technique frequently, and avoided the smoothing problems of "plastering" the entire wall or ceiling. My method was as follows. Using a 12-inch wide wallboard taping knife, I applied the thinned wallboard compound in stripes across the wall or ceiling. These stripes or bands of compound were applied 12 inches wide (the width of the taping knife) and about 10 inches apart. When the first bands or stripes of compound were dry, I went back and troweled another band of compound in the blank areas between the first stripes of compound, completing the coat of compound over the entire wall or ceiling surface. This technique allows you to get a smooth coat, with little sanding, and can renew even old plaster surfaces. Rather than trying to remove texture patterns you are tired of, skim coating is also an option for covering over an unattractive textured surface. The technique is to scrape away any high "bumps" in the texture paint, then trowel a coat or two of wallboard compound over the entire surface, covering up the texture pattern. Because the rough texture makes it difficult to trowel, you may choose to hire a professional wallboard taper or plasterer to skim coat over texture paint.

Most modern patch products can be painted over the same day, so no waiting is needed. Any water-based patching material can be painted immediately (when the material is set but not dry) using latex paint. Electric heat gun can be used to speed set or drying of patching material. Photo by the author.

5
Removing an Interior Wall

For any of a number of reasons you may wish to remove a wall in your house. You may want to remove the wall between the master bedroom and an unused bedroom to enlarge the master suite. Or you might want to combine the floor space of a small bedroom with a bathroom to create an extended bathroom, a spa, a bathing lounge, or an exercise room. Before starting to remove a wall, check first to see if the wall is a bearing (load-bearing) wall.

Many texts warn that it is difficult to tell whether a wall is load-bearing or non-bearing. It should not be difficult, if you understand framing procedure, to separate the two types of wall. In most cases, you can simply note the location of the wall and check to see what is directly above that may be supported by the wall you wish to remove.

From a structural standpoint there are only two types of walls. The first type of wall supports not only its own weight but the weight of another floor, or the roof, above it. These walls are called "load-bearing" walls. The second type of wall is a partition or curtain that divides available floor space, and supports only its own weight. This type of wall is called "non-bearing."

Before roof trusses were developed, houses were framed or stick-built one board at a time, and the ceiling joists and roof rafters of these houses are supported by walls that bear the roof load, called

"load-bearing" walls. Walls that merely served as privacy screens or curtain walls, walls that define room perimeters but do not support any weight except their own, are called "non-bearing" walls. Most walls that are parallel to the direction of the floor or ceiling joists are not load-bearing, and are easily removed.

Before removing any interior wall it is important to determine whether that wall supports any load above it, such as a second story or roof. Non-bearing walls can be removed without any concern for the structure of the house, but you must provide some alternate means of support, such as a beam(s) if you remove a wall that is carrying a load — another floor or the roof — above it.

In all houses, regardless of their roof construction, the long exterior walls (walls that are perpendicular to the joists) are load-bearing, meaning they hold up the weight of any upper floors plus the weight of the roof structure, whether it is stick-built or truss-built. In stick-built houses, or those with no roof trusses, the end walls of the house (the walls that are parallel to the floor and ceiling joists) are also load-bearing, meaning they hold up the gable or hip, plus the roof weight. If the roof is trussed, the gable ends likewise are trussed, so the end walls of the house are not load-bearing.

If there is a wall or beam down the center of the house, as seen from the basement or crawl space, the center wall or beam is load-bearing, and it carries the weight of the floor above. You can see the ends of the floor joists where they overlap atop the beam or center wall top plate. If there is a center wall down the middle of the first floor of a single-story house, and the roof is not trussed, that center wall is load-bearing and carries the roof above. If the house is multi-story, the center wall of the first floor is supporting the weight of the second floor. If there is also a center wall down the middle of the second (or subsequent) floor, and the roof above is not truss construction, the center wall is load-bearing, carrying the weight of the roof structure above. If the roof is built of trusses, called clear-span trusses, all the weight of the roof is supported by the exterior walls of the house, and even the center wall is non-bearing, meaning it serves only as a curtain or partition to divide the space.

If you determine that the wall you wish to remove is load-bearing, it is best to call in a professional to do the work. Even if you recognize the need for a substitute support beam or wall, it will be difficult for the beginner to determine just how much support is needed. For example, the size of beam required to replace a bearing wall depends on the load or actual weight to be supported, plus the length of the span over which the weight is distributed. Failure to supply enough support for the load may result in catastrophe, such as extensive structural damage to the house or personal injury to the occupants.

If you have a friend or a contractor you can call on, it is wise to ask his/her advice before deciding to remove any wall. You want to be very sure of what you are doing to avoid doing harm to yourself and possibly doing extensive and expensive damage to your house. Never take a chance: to avoid serious consequences, know positively what you are doing before you begin.

REMOVING A NON-BEARING WALL

At this point you're sure that the wall in question is non-bearing, so no structural problems will arise from removing it. There may be other problems

with wall construction, and now is the time to determine what those problems may be.

Check the location of drain and vent plumbing pipes to be sure there are none in the wall you want to remove. It is both difficult and expensive to relocate drain and vent plumbing pipes, so check from the attic side and the basement side to be sure there are no surprises hidden in the wall you want to remove.

Next, check the wall for electrical outlets. By today's electrical codes, the wall outlets must be no more than 12 feet apart, so any wall should have at least one electrical outlet to remove. Note that there will be an electrical outlet on *both* sides of the wall, so plan accordingly.

To avoid potential shock from handling or cutting into live or "hot" electrical wires, never cut into a wall until you have shut off the electrical supply to the circuit that includes the electrical outlets.

When you have determined that the wall to be removed is non-bearing, removing the wall is actually a very simple — if dusty — matter. You will need a crowbar, a hammer, a handsaw (maybe), and a reciprocating saw with a hacksaw blade (can be rented; useful for cutting through framing nails for dismantling wall studs and plates). For personal protection wear a work cap (a hard hat if you are removing ceilings) and a dust mask and eye goggles.

Dismantling a wall is a dirty business at best: wear clothes that cover you completely. Wear a long-sleeved work shirt that buttons at the neck and wrists to shut out the dirt and dust. You might also wear an oversized bandanna tied around your collar, cowboy style, as extra protection against dust. Wear goggles to protect your eyes from plaster and wallboard particles, sawdust, and steel nail fragments.

Work gloves will save a thousand splinters, blisters, and possible cuts from handling removed materials. The most durable gloves for demolition work are leather work gloves. Also, removed plaster lath and wallboard may contain rusty nails that can be a hazard to feet. Wear heavy-soled work shoes, not hazard to feet. Wear heavy-soled work shoes, not tennis shoes, when working around a construction site. Over-the-ankle work boots with heavy soles not only protect against nails in the feet but provide ankle support to prevent sprained ankles and to protect feet from injury when climbing ladders.

Keep trash cans handy and deposit materials in the cans as soon as you remove them. Waste materials that are permitted to pile up on the floors interfere with work progress, present a tripping hazard, and prolong that dusty, messy period of the remodeling job. A mess is less disagreeable if you clean it up as quickly as possible.

Removing Plastered Walls

Removing plaster from a wall or ceiling can be a particularly dirty and dusty job. Shut the forced air furnace off or turn the thermostat down to prevent plaster dust from being picked up and circulated through the house via air ducts. Use 2-inch wide masking tape to tape polyethylene plastic sheets over any doors, to keep plaster dust from drifting into adjacent rooms. Keep a pair of street shoes at the entry of the work area and change into your work shoes when you enter or leave the work area. This will minimize tracking the dust throughout the house.

Old plaster that has deteriorated tends to crumble and break up as it is removed, increasing the dust factor. Use a mason's chisel to cut the plaster in a clean, straight line at all wall and ceiling corners. This avoids cracking the plaster on surfaces adjacent to the areas to be removed. Tips for minimizing dust and cleanup include pulling the plaster off in as large chunks as possible. If plaster is loose, try to insert a prybar in a crack and pry large chunks of plaster off the wall. As the chunks loosen, pry with the bar and grasp the plaster pieces with your free hand. As soon as the piece is freed from the wall, place it in the trash container. If you let the plaster chunks fall to the floor as they are pried free from the lath, the plaster will break up and create a dust mess. Wear the eye goggles and dust mask to minimize your exposure to the dust.

When the plaster is removed, use a prybar to remove the plaster lath. This step also will raise a lot of dust, as the keys break loose from the wood lath. Pry the wood lath away intact if possible, to minimize the debris and keep it in a large size that can be handled more easily. Be careful of the rusty nails as you pry the lath off. The nails present a hazard to both hands and feet, and tetanus can result from puncture wounds. Be sure your tetanus shots are up to date before doing demolition work.

When you have removed the wood lath from the studs, use a shop vacuum to pick up all dust. This step will keep the dust contained in the work area, with limited opportunity for it to spread through the house.

The next step is to remove any electrical outlet boxes and wire. Be sure the circuit is dead, shut off at the supply panel via the breakers or fuses, to avoid electrical shock. Use a slot screwdriver to release the wire from the receptacle screws, and use a prybar to pry the boxes loose from the studs. Set the boxes and receptacles aside if you intend to reuse them.

With the plaster and lath already removed, all the framing studs are exposed for easy removal. Studs are joined to the top and sole wall plates via nails. The studs can usually be removed by hitting the ends of the studs, driving the studs sideways and loose from the nails that hold them to the top and sole plates. You can remove the studs by striking either the top or bottom end first. Often, if one end of a stud is freed by pounding it out with the hammer, you can remove the stud by pulling outward and twisting it to free the opposite end of the stud.

Remove all the wall studs and set them aside. All that remains is to remove the top and sole plates. Because the wall top and sole plates were in place before the wall was plastered, there will be a bare channel along both side walls and across the ceiling. When you remove the sole plate there will also be a void in the flooring, where the old sole plate has flooring and plaster walls and ceilings, you must patch the holes in the plaster and in the flooring.

If the existing flooring is carpeting, vinyl floor covering, or tile (either ceramic tile or vinyl floor tile), the gap or channel in the floor can be filled with plywood cut to fit the width of the void. Then the carpet, floor covering, or tile can be redone to suit.

Tongue-and-groove hardwood flooring is more difficult to patch. The best approach is to have a professional come in and remove part of the flooring, patching in strips so the end joints are staggered. If you try to cut pieces to fit in the void the end joints will be unsightly, and the floor will naturally have a patched look. A professional floor layer can patch the floor so the patching cannot be detected, so it is worth the cost to have it professionally done.

One precaution before you begin patching the plaster: in plaster construction the inside corners are finished with a corner tool called a *plow*. Often, the corner tool will leave a rounded corner rather than a square one. The problem is that, when you remove the old wall, there are ridges along both sides of the void where side studs and top and sole plates interrupted the plaster. If you just trowel a fill coat of plaster over these ridges, you will have a "bump" or high spot in the plaster, and the patched area will be very visible when it is painted. To avoid making an unsightly plaster patch, use a level or other straightedge to be sure there are no ridges along the edges of these perimeter channels in the plaster. If there are ridges in the old plaster, use a portable grinder to grind the edges of the voids down, so they are level with the surrounding plaster. Then continue with the repair process.

To patch the plaster walls and ceiling gaps, use staples or hot glue to secure metal (wire) lath in the voids. Coat the edges of the plaster and the wire lath with latex bonding liquid, and fill the voids with patch plaster to about one-half their depth. Use an old hair comb to make furrows in the wet patching plaster. This step, called "scarifying," roughens the first plaster coat so the second or finishing coat of plaster will bond to the first coat. Let the first coat of plaster set, then mix a fresh batch of patching plaster and give the repair areas another coat of plaster, leveling this coat with the existing plaster. Let the plaster cure, prime the repair areas, and paint.

Removing Walls with Wallboard

Walls finished with wallboard require less effort and cleanup to remove. The wallboard will usually come off in large chunks, creating little dust and mess. In fact, if you use a sidelight (a bare light bulb held against the wall at night) to locate the nail or screw sites, you can use a nail set to drive the fasteners through the wallboard and take the wallboard down in large sheets.

When the wallboard has been removed from the framing, proceed with the wall dismantling as noted in the plaster section above. Take apart the electrical wiring, and pry loose the flanges on the air supply or return ducts, if any. Then knock out the studs, and pry out the end wall studs plus the top and sole wall plates.

To fill any gaps in the wallboard, sand down any ridges along the channels where the studs or plates were removed. Then cut filler strips of wallboard and place them in the channels. Tape and finish these wallboard fillers as you would finish any wallboard joint (see Chapter 3, Finishing Wallboard).

6
Interior Painting

Interior painting is by a wide margin the most common do-it-yourself activity. About 95 percent of homeowners do at least some of their own interior painting and patching. When I was senior editor of a home magazine called *The Family Handyman*, we conducted informal reader surveys to learn the readership of our feature stories. Any story that concerned interior painting invariably got top marks for popularity with our readers.

With all the instructional painting material that has been developed for the consumer, one would think that all the painting problems had been solved. In fact, there is a wide gap in information available on the most common interior painting problems. As a guest expert on various talk radio shows, I get a steady flow of calls from people with paint problems. The calls included such problems as:

• I painted my spray-textured ceilings and the paint is uneven, full of roller marks. How come?

• I painted the interior trim and sash on my windows and now I can't open them. What happened?

• I just painted my entry door. How can I get paint smears off my door hardware?

• I painted the concrete floor in my basement laundry room, and the paint is peeling. What did I do wrong? What should I do now?

You get the idea. I have come to believe that the problem arises at least in part from the erroneous belief that "anyone can paint." This belief that "painting is simple" has been fostered by paint manufacturers who run advertisements to convince us that painting a room is like a stroll in the park. One ad makes the premise that company is coming for dinner, and the roast is already in the oven. Maybe we should redecorate the living room. The next frame shows the couch draped with a sheet, and the couple are busily painting the room. Now, you and I manage to get paint on *everything*, but not Mr. and Mrs. D-I-Y'er. He is wearing a pair of slacks, dress shoes, and a sport shirt, while she is dressed to go shopping. In a brief but enjoyable interlude they complete the redecoration, hang Grandma's picture back on the wall, and greet their dinner guests without having even to wash their hands. Is that the way you remember your last paint job? More than a little unrealistic, but still we see this simplified picture of home painting. The paint "flows on smoothly" is "drip-free" and features "easy cleanup with soap and warm water." It is no wonder that if you attempt to advise people on their painting they tend to shrug off any advice you give. After all, *everyone* knows how to paint. Well, as Sportin' Life once observed, "It ain't necessarily so." In this chapter we will attempt to help you solve the mysteries of interior painting. Even though you may have done a lot of interior painting, remember the premise of this book. There may be a number of different ways to accomplish a task, but there is always a *best way* to do anything, so listen up and we'll try to convince you that our way is the best way.

PAINTING CEILINGS

Tools

For painting ceilings you will need a 9-inch paint roller and a paint brush for cutting in corners. Use a medium-fleece roller cover for applying flat paints to smooth ceiling surfaces, and a long-fleece roller cover for painting over rough or textured surfaces. Note we never recommend using the short-fleece roller covers that are offered for applying flat paint to smooth surfaces. A medium roller cover will carry more paint to the surface and will leave fewer edge marks in the paint than a short-fleece roller cover.

Buy a quality roller and spin the shaft with your hand to be sure it moves easily and does not bind. Buy a roller with a threaded handle, so you can screw in an extension handle that lets you paint the ceiling without scaffold, while standing on the floor. The extension paint roller handle is known in the paint trade as an "idiot stick."

Most texts recommend a narrow brush for cutting paint at corners, but most pros use a 4-inch brush for cutting in corners. Why the wider brush? The width of the bristle helps to stabilize the brush and hold it from turning in the corners. Most pros feel you can cut a straighter and cleaner corner with a wider brush. If you haven't tried it, by all means do so: a wider brush cuts better than a narrow brush. Choose a brush with bristles of flagged nylon or a nylon/polyester blend for most paint applications, whether you are applying alkyd (oil) or water-base paint. Use pure (animal, usually hog) bristle brushes for applying fine oil finishes on woodwork or trim, because pure bristle brushes leave fewer brush marks.

Even though you use an extension handle in the roller and stand on the floor to paint, you will need a 4- to 6-foot stepladder. Use the stepladder to reach, mask, and cut in the ceiling/wall corners. Note that ladders are rated on their labels for the amount of weight they will safely hold. Don't buy a cheap household stepladder with 200-pound weight limits if you play tackle for the Chicago Bears.

You will also need a supply of sheet polyethylene plastic and a supply of 2-inch wide masking tape. The 8-foot wide plastic sheets (or roll plastic) can be taped to the wall at the corners of the ceiling, and will protect the walls, windows and Grandma's picture from paint splatters while you are rolling the ceiling. Pro painters use the wider 2-inch masking tape because you can stick the top edge of the wide tape at the top of the corner and leave the bottom edge of the tape curled outward. Then unroll the plastic sheets and insert the top edge of the plastic under the bottom edge of the masking tape. Press the bottom edge of the masking tape tight to the plastic sheets and let the sheets drape down the wall, covering and protecting the entire wall and base trim.

For covering floors use a canvas drop cloth. Plastic floor covers are slippery to walk on, and are so light that they will not stay in place. Any paint spatters that fall on plastic sheets will stay wet forever, and you will pick them up on your shoe soles and track them about. Painter's canvas drop cloths soak up spills and spatters, so they dry quickly. The canvas drop cloths are not expensive, when you consider the years of use they will return. I have a drop cloth that is 25 feet x 15 feet, and I paid about $30 for it at a painter's supply store eight years ago. It will cover most any floor completely and can be folded over for use in smaller rooms. I've loaned it to many people who were painting, have used it to redecorate my entire house, and it will outlast me. It is a good investment, providing the best floor protection plus safety under foot.

Choosing the Paint

The ceiling is the largest unbroken surface in the house. It is not broken up or interrupted by furniture placement, draperies, or window or door openings, as walls are. The ceiling is also subjected to unflattering lighting, either from flush-mounted fixtures that subject the ceiling to critical sidelighting

Sand texture paints can be applied with a roller. The light sand texture offers decorating variety plus good hiding power to cover minor blemishes. Photo courtesy USG.

Full range of available textures include the light sand texture of the walls and the heavy spray texture pattern on the ceiling. Spray textures such as those used on most residential ceilings have no sealing power: you must first seal them with an alkyd sealer, then roll on a coat of new latex ceiling paint. Photo courtesy of USG.

or from reflected daylight. Ceilings also present an uninterrupted plane for visual inspection, and thus will readily show any bulges, waves, or defects. All these factors combine to make the ceiling the most critical paint surface in the house.

Because texture paints are tooled into a rough surface, they break up the light reflection that tends to emphasize any defects. Also, texture paints are made to have a flat finish, or lack of *sheen*. Sheen is the term used to indicate the gloss or degree of light reflection of a paint surface. So for ceiling surfaces you want a paint that has a texture and a totally flat sheen.

It is this combination of qualities — a rough finish to break up lighting and a low-sheen or a no-sheen finish — that created the popularity of spray texture ceilings. In addition to finding the spray texture effect an appealing one, spray texture also enhances the appearance of the ceiling and conceals minor blemishes in the wallboard or plaster surface.

Note, however, that, like most products, texture paint has been badly oversold as a problem-solver. You cannot *paint* a ceiling or wall to make it flat: you must start with a good plaster or wallboard job to end up with an attractive textured ceiling. Also, for reasons we discussed in Chapter 4, Patching Walls and Ceilings, structural cracks will reopen when temperature and humidity cause movement in the framing or structure. It should be obvious that no paint finish will permanently seal open cracks in a ceiling or wall. These must be repaired before applying texture paint. If you ever find a paint, texture or otherwise, that will perform to flatten an uneven surface, or will seal cracks permanently, contact me immediately. I guarantee I will make at least three people filthy rich with the product: you, me, and whoever owns the product. Be sure any surface to be painted is sound, clean, and free of cracks before you begin to paint. Use texture paint to gain a desirable texture finish while covering up very minor surface flaws.

Texture paints are difficult to apply, for pros as well

as for the novice. First, the paste consistency of the material makes it difficult to spread evenly and to pattern uniformly. Unlike ordinary paint, texture paint must first be evenly applied over the surface, then it must be worked into a desired pattern. This two-stage application means that the paint must be kept "open" or workable for a longer period of time. It is advisable that you work with a partner when applying texture paint: one person can apply the material and spread it, the other can use a tool to pattern or texture the paint.

The best bet for texture painting is to hire professionals to do the job. If you decide to do the work yourself, there are a number of steps you can take to make the job easier. The goal is to keep the texture paint from drying so that you (and your partner) will have time to spread the paint and pattern it.

Steps to help you get a good job with texture include the following. First, a texture paint must take and hold a pattern. Do not thin texture paints, because they will flow out and lose their pattern while drying. Choose a ready-mix latex-base texture product, and note the spread rate on the label. Whereas ordinary paint may cover 350 to 400 square feet of surface per gallon, texture paints may cover only 50-100 square feet per gallon. Texture paints can be expensive because they don't provide much coverage per gallon.

If you've never done texture painting, stay away from the powder texture products that must be mixed with water. Some of these powder texture products are excellent, and pros prefer to mix their own texture paint. But inadequate mixing or mixing with the wrong water/powder ratio can ruin the product or result in a poor texture job. Likewise, it is best to concentrate on getting the texture paint on the wall in an attractive pattern and not to worry about the color. Many premixed latex texture products are available in colors, but our advice is to apply a white texture paint to suit, then paint over it to get a desired color other than white. Use a flat latex paint to paint over texture finishes.

Paints dry in two ways. First, the water from the latex paint evaporates into the air. Also, the water from the paint will soak into the surface to which it is applied. To control the drying process you must take steps to control both these types of drying.

Before starting to texture, apply an alkyd primer to the wall or ceiling and let the primer dry at least twenty-four hours before proceeding to the texture application. The alkyd primer will seal the surface so that water from the texture paint cannot soak into the surface and speed drying time. To retard the rate of evaporation, choose a painting day that is not too warm and dry. If you are painting during the cold weather, turn the furnace thermostat down to keep room temperature cool and to avoid drafts from air movement by forced air furnaces. Close the room off to avoid drafts from other areas, and place a humidifier in the room to raise the humidity levels. This will slow drying time of the texture and extend open time so you have time to achieve the desired texture pattern.

The easiest texture pattern is a stipple texture, done with rollers. To achieve this light texture, one person uses a long-fleece (nap) roller to apply the texture paint and to spread it evenly over the surface. Then the helper, also equipped with a long-fleece roller, moves over the wet texture paint, leaving the desired pattern. The rollers are always moved in the same direction when the pattern is being established, so that the pattern appears continuous and uniform.

Other texture patterns can be achieved using scraps of carpeting, sponges, paint brushes, or even whisk brooms to make a variety of patterns. And, of course, the most popular ceiling texture is sprayed on using air equipment. Because of the nature of the equipment required, and the degree of skill required, spray texturing is not for amateurs. You will have to look at the results for as long as you own the home; you don't want to foul up the job. If you want ceilings spray textured, hire a professional.

Painting Spray-Textured Ceilings

One of the most difficult jobs for the homeowner is painting over an existing spray texture finish. Most people make the mistake of trying to paint over the texture using a paint roller. They first buy a cheap grade of latex paint, roll it over the texture, and end up with a streaked mess, showing many roller marks and uneven or blotchy paint distribution.

What is the key for refurbishing textured ceilings? First, consider having the ceilings resprayed by pros. The pros will come in, cover all the walls and floors with polyethylene plastic, and will respray the ceilings. In many urban areas you can get the work done by Sears. If you want an alternate bid, or Sears does not perform the work in your area, seek out a wallboard (drywall) contractor or painter to respray your ceilings.

If you want to paint over the spray-textured ceiling, the long fleece roller is the right tool for the job. But spray-texture materials are *mill mixes*, meaning they are a mixture of powdered vinyl plus aggregates such as Styrofoam or perlite that form the "bumps" in the texture. The applicator just mixes these powder/aggregate materials with water and sprays them on the ceilings. Obviously, the texture finish is not sealed, so it presents a highly absorbent surface to be painted. To apply paint to this texture material is not unlike trying to paint a sponge: there will be a high degree of paint absorption. And because the paint is quickly absorbed into the material, the painter cannot spread the paint evenly over the surface, hence the splotchy coverage and the roller marks on the ceiling.

To paint over a spray-textured ceiling, you must first apply a coat of alkyd primer. The primer will seal the texture so that there is no paint absorption, and the paint will lie evenly on the surface. Because there is no paint absorption you can roll the paint out, getting even paint distribution, so the finish coat will have a clean, uniform appearance.

Roll a clear concrete sealer on garage or basement floors that are not finished. Sealer prevents spilled materials from staining concrete slabs, prevents dusting of the concrete surface. Photo by the author.

For a return to a flat paint finish, try removal of existing texture. Then trowel one or more skim coats of wallboard compound over the entire surface, wet sand, and paint as desired. Photo by the author.

When you have applied the alkyd primer, use the long-fleece roller to apply the finish coat. Keep in mind that the texture pattern is already established, and all you must do is provide a new finish coat. Choose a dead flat latex paint for your ceiling. You want the paint to have little or no sheen or gloss, so be sure the paint is the flattest finish available. Many paint manufacturers make a paint especially formulated for use on ceilings. Such paints will be labelled "ceiling" or "ceiling flat white," and these are the paints you should choose for painting your ceilings. If you can't find such a product, ask your paint dealer to recommend a paint for you.

Painting Ceiling (Acoustic) Tile
Acoustic tiles have a soft finish to help them absorb sound waves. If you apply a coat of ordinary flat paint to the acoustic tiles you will reduce the acoustic value of the tiles. Instead, consider cleaning the soiled acoustic tile using wallpaper dough (a soft material, like play dough, used to clean wall covering). Or check in the Yellow Pages of your phone book under Janitorial Services & Supplies. There are cleaning companies that specialize in cleaning acoustic tile ceilings.

If you do choose to paint acoustic tile, choose a flat latex product and thin it to the maximum degree indicated on the paint label. Then use a roller with a long fleece to paint the tiles.

PAINTING WALLS

In the past decade latex paint has become the standard for painting any interior surface. Tough new acrylic latex formulas produce products that are not only easy to apply and to clean up during application, they are tough and durable in service. Interior latex paints are now available with any degree of sheen or gloss, right up to high gloss finishes that once were possible to achieve only by using oil or enamel paints. Because latex paints do not contain harmful chemical vehicles, and are thinned and cleaned with water only, they are also favored for their reduced impact on the environment.

Latex paints are commonly used for painting ceilings, walls, trim, and even for concrete floors. The only place left in interior painting where many pros still prefer alkyd paints is for painting furniture and cabinetry. Latex paints may leave a "softer" finish that may contribute to sticking cabinet doors or drawers, so use alkyd paints for these purposes.

For painting most walls, the best material choice is a flat acrylic latex. As discussed earlier in the Ceiling section, a flat paint reflects less light and minimizes any defects in the wall. Using a medium-fleece roller to apply wall paint will leave the paint with a light stipple texture finish, and this slight texture also helps to break up lighting and improve the appearance of the wall.

Before starting to paint a wall, inspect the wall for popped nails, cracks, and water damage. Make repairs as set forth in Chapter 4, Patching Walls and Ceilings. If the wall appears blemish-free, lightly sand the old paint to remove any lint or dirt that might have clung to the old paint finish. Run your hand over the surface to be sure it feels smooth and blemish-free.

No matter how professional the results of your paint job, any cracks between wall and trim will look dark and therefore dirty. Before painting, check for gaps between the wall and trim or cabinetry. Use a latex caulk to fill any cracks, and tool the caulk with a wetted finger. Filling any cracks will make the paint job look tight and workmanlike.

When painting corners where walls meet textured ceilings, a common problem is cutting against the bumps of the rough texture. The brush will bounce or wiggle as it is drawn over the bumps in the texture, making a squiggly paint line between the wall and ceiling. This uneven line can be very objectionable and can make your paint job look amateurish. How to cut a straight line at the wall/ceiling corner? Remember that the aggregate—the material that makes those bumps in texture — is very soft. Place the tip of a taping knife at the juncture of the wall and ceiling, and, holding the knife at a 30-45 degree angle to the wall, scrape away the bumps so that there is a clean, smooth groove at the wall/ceiling line. Don't fight the bumps when painting — scrape them away.

Some walls in the house are subject to frequent soiling and moisture attack. For these walls choose a latex paint with a high gloss, or even a high gloss alkyd enamel paint. These high gloss paints are easier to clean, and they resist moisture and dirt penetration. Use them in the kitchen, bathroom, or laundry room to make a longer-lasting, moisture-resistant paint finish. Use high gloss paint in any high traffic area such as halls, stairways, or children's bedrooms or playrooms.

PAINTING NEW WALLBOARD

New wallboard presents a crosshatch pattern where screws, joints, and corner beads are treated with taping compound. These areas of compound are interrupted by areas of bare wallboard face paper. The result is that when you are painting wallboard you are in fact painting two different materials — taping compound and bare paper — so it should not be surprising when the painted wallboard walls look as though they have a checkerboard pattern. For years the wallboard industry has sought some means of ending this difference in materials. The technical term is that they are trying to equalize the pattern and the suction over the entire surface of the wallboard.

When used as a first coat on new wallboard, oil or alkyd primers or sealers are a disaster. The slow-drying oil-base products raise the nap of the face paper on the wallboard, and then these raised fibers are locked into the drying paint. The result is that any area treated with compound will look and feel smooth, while the areas where face paper is left bare will have a rough textured feel and look. The fact is that the Gypsum Association and wallboard manufacturers have *never* recommended using alkyd primers as a first coat over wallboard that is to be painted or papered. The sole exception to this statement is that an alkyd primer *is* recommended for

priming wallboard ceilings that will be finished with a water-base spray texture.

For the first or prime coat over new wallboard, the industry standard is to use a coat of heavy-bodied latex paint. This heavy-bodied paint will help equalize the suction over the wallboard surface and will also help even out the texture of the surface where smooth compound meets the rough face paper of the wallboard.

Even though wallboard is properly treated with a first coat of latex paint, wallboard construction is still subject to joint flashing or joint shadowing, where the areas treated with compound appear darker than areas of bare paper. To overcome this, the gypsum industry has long recommended that the entire wallboard area be coated with a shear ("shear" as in "*shear* off the compound" not "sheer" as in thin) or skim coat of compound, to help relieve the differences presented by trying to decorate two different building materials (taping compound and wallboard face paper).

The ultimate treatment for ending suction and texture problems on new wallboard is to use a new product called First Coat. First Coat is a latex product, available mixed as paint or in a powder form that can be mixed with water. First Coat is a product of United States Gypsum (USG). USG is the company that invented wallboard, and the trade name for this product is Sheetrock®. First Coat overcomes all the failures of using ordinary primers or sealers as a first coat over wallboard. It fills the textured surface of the paper so that the texture appears uniform, while sealing the face so that paint suction is absorbed equally over the entire surface. To ensure a proper base coat for wallboard and to be sure of getting a quality paint job, you must begin with proper preparation. This means that you should use First Coat to overcome the inherent problems associated with wallboard construction. If you simply cannot find a supplier, you can ask any paint store to special order First Coat, or contact United States Gypsum for the name of the dealer nearest you.

Completing re-finish of old textured surface. Photo by author.

USING MASKING TAPE

Masking tape is available in a variety of widths for use on any paint application. A number of companies make masking tape: my brand choice is 3M, which pioneered in the protective tape business and makes a superior product. My preference for Scotch Brand tapes developed when I was finishing and painting wallboard for a living. Because of the sanding process on wallboard there is always a layer of compound dust on everything, and most tapes will not stick to the dusty surfaces. I soon learned to remove as much dust as possible from any surface to be protected, before applying the masking tape.

To remove dust from new wallboard, wipe the surface with a wet sponge. To remove dust from trim, use a tack cloth (available at most paint stores) to pick up the dust. When painting wood trim or cabinetry, use a liquid sander product to avoid making dust with sandpaper. Even though you may try to remove dust so it will not interfere with getting a good bond between the masking tape and the surface you want to protect, some dust may remain in a construction or repair environment. I've found that Scotch Brand or 3M tapes provide superior adhesion on problem surfaces, so I always specify 3M masking tape.

One problem when using masking tape is that loose tape lets paint run or drip under the edge of the tape. These runs are difficult to remove. To be sure you have a tight bond on the edge of masking tape, first use sandpaper or steel wool to remove any bumps of dirt or lint from the surface to be taped. The small bumps prevent the tape from sticking uniformly and stopping paint runs. When you are sure the old paint is smooth where you will apply the masking tape, apply the tape carefully, being sure you tape in a straight line. Then use the tip of a putty knife to press the edge of the masking tape tight against the surface you will protect. This ensures a tight edge seal between the tape and the surface to be protected, and will prevent most paint runs.

Another key tip when using masking tape is to remove the tape as soon as the paint has dried enough so it will not run. Many people leave masking tape on until the paint has hardened. Paint will soak into the masking tape and will stick to the taped surface. This hardened paint can so bond the tape to the protected surface that the tape will be very difficult to remove. Pull the tape away before the paint is completely dry to ensure easy tape removal. Another plus of early masking tape removal is that any paint runs that have managed to seep under the tape will be easier to clean off while the paint is still soft.

PAINTING CONCRETE FLOORS

Most paint jobs that fail do so because of lack of proper preparation. Any surface to be painted should be cleaned and free of dirt, mildew, grease, oil, soap, and wax. Any of these compounds will interfere with the bond between the new paint and the surface to be painted.

A concrete floor can present especially tough problems as a subject for paint. The concrete floor remains cooler than the air or other materials around it, and therefore humidity can condense and form moisture on the concrete surface. This humidity must be controlled in the basement or other area, both during the painting process and later, to protect the finished surface. Concrete floors that are attacked by water seepage or are constantly damp

from humidity will not hold paint. Drying up the problem may mean installing gutters on the house, adding dirt along the basement walls to improve the grade or slope of the lawn, so water can run away, and patching cracks in the walls or floors to block water entry — all are possible steps to take to dry up a basement floor.

Controlling humidity can be done by opening basement windows or using a fan to increase air circulation. This may seem an elemental approach, but I am always amazed to inspect a damp basement, only to find that the basement windows are painted shut and have not been opened for thirty years. One mistake is to open only one window: no air flow can exist unless the air can flow in one window, through the basement, and flow out an open window or a vent at the other end.

To paint a floor, first clean it thoroughly with an appropriate cleaner. Trisodium phosphate (TSP) is available at most paint stores in dry or powder form and can be mixed with water in varying proportions to make a mild to strong cleaner. Odorless mineral spirits will remove wax, grease, and oil. Your local janitorial supply store can recommend the right solvent to clean any chemical from the concrete floor.

If the concrete floor has been troweled extremely smooth, use a concrete etcher such as UGL Drylok Etch to roughen the surface slightly. Concrete floors that are dusting can be sealed with a product such as UGL's Clear Concrete Protector. Use a paint deglosser or sandpaper to dull the gloss finish on concrete floors with a shiny paint coating. Use a primer to prime any bare spots on painted concrete floors. Then apply a paint that is specifically formulated for use on concrete floors. Note that because of the characteristics needed for a good floor paint, such as resistance to abrasive wear, ordinary paint will not last and should not be used for concrete floors. Use a special product, such as UGL's Drylok Concrete Floor Paint (latex) for painting concrete floors.

PAINTING POTPOURRI

If you will ask your paint supplier to name his worst problem with customer complaints, he will tell you that people should "read the directions on the label." Because most of us think that painting is a simple job, we assume that all latex paints are alike, all alkyd paints are alike, and that we can save painting chores to do on our vacation, or on a day off, never mind the weather conditions on our chosen day. You should always read and heed label directions for using the particular product you have chosen.

Directions that are often ignored include:

- Surfaces to be painted must be properly cleaned and prepared for painting. Paint simply will not adhere to dirt, oil, wax, and other impurities that lie on a paint surface.

- Keep in mind the spread rate, or rate of paint application. I have heard homeowners brag that they covered 600 square feet with a paint that promised only 300 to 400 square feet of coverage. How would you, as a manufacturer, like to cover the warranties for durability and washability on a product that was applied only half as thick as directed?

- Take into account temperature and humidity conditions. People regularly assume that the manufacturer did not *really* mean his advice not to apply paint at temperatures colder than 50 degrees or warmer than 80 degrees.

- Don't mix old paint with new in an attempt to "use up" leftover paint. Use leftover paint in a closet, or mix several portions of leftover latex paint together (you will probably end up with "builders' beige") and use it in a garage or utility room. Or donate the leftover paint to a charity, if you have a half-gallon or more. Less than half-gallon quantities are not generally useful for wall paint. Lesser amounts of paint can sometimes be donated to theater groups for use in painting stage sets. *Don't* mix old shelf paint with new paint and risk contamination of the new material.

7
Lighting for Effect

If you experiment with interior decorating, you will learn to appreciate the dramatic role that proper lighting plays in design. In other chapters we have discussed such topics as patching and repairing walls and ceilings, the importance of straight framing, proper wallboard installation, and the light reflective qualities of various sheens of paint. But it can honestly be said that, if you want to improve the appearance of your home's interior, the one step you can take that will have the greatest effect is to replace bright, critical light fixtures with fixtures that enhance the beauty of your walls, ceilings, and floors. You can use the straightest lumber, hire the best workmen, buy the best materials, and still your walls and ceilings will look like a washboard if you have light fixtures that do not flatter your interior.

Would you like a dramatic demonstration of the importance of proper lighting? Wait until darkness falls, then remove the shade or reflector from a lamp or mechanic's trouble light. With all other lights turned off, hold the bare, lighted bulb about 6 inches from any wall or ceiling. Now move the bare lighted bulb about, always staying close to the wall or ceiling so that the surface is sidelighted, or subjected to parallel light beams. The defects in the surface will come out like stars at night: you will be able to count every bump, valley, dent, pimple, or crack in that surface. Direct sidelighting will bring out and maximize all the irregularities and defects on that surface. If you want to make a surface look its worst, subject it to strong sidelighting.

Now before you bring a lawsuit against your plasterer or your wallboard contractor for bad work-

manship, go into your dark garage and subject your family limousine to the same harsh sidelighting. No matter if your chariot was built by fine Italian coach makers, when the sheet metal panels are subjected to sidelighting, the car will look as though it has been driven over a cliff.

Why is sidelighting so critical on a surface? Because light beams travel in a straight line. If the surface over which the light beams move is perfectly in plane, meaning it is perfectly flat, the sidelight will not cast any shadows and will show the surface for what it is: perfect. But because perfection is hard to come by in this imperfect world, most wall or ceiling surfaces have dings, dents, pimples, and bumps that will cause shadows when subjected to sidelighting. If you move the light away from the surface so it is not sidelighted, all the shadows and thus the "defects," disappear. The plasterer is again the master craftsman we first thought him to be. All that was changed was the light.

The obvious, if neglected, lesson is to avoid sidelighting any surface in the home. The point is that we would not display our car or other possessions in the harshest possible light. But for reasons of style or pure stubbornness, people will often insist that they retain some favorite lamp or fixture, even though the harsh light from the blasted fixture makes the wall look like a washboard.

Our point is that if we would never show our other most-favored possessions in their worst light, by the same token we should replace unflattering room lighting with lighting that is both more useful and less critical on interior surfaces.

A great example of critical lighting that was once very popular is the infamous pole lamp. In the '60s, every tract home in the known world had at least one of those multi-bulb monstrosities, making life miserable for the painter, the plasterer, and the wallboard contractor. These tradesmen would do their level best to make the living room walls as flat as a pool table. The painter would dutifully apply a nice flat or low-sheen latex paint to the walls, and a texture paint to the ceiling. Both these finishes were intended to make the joints and nail holes in the wallboard invisible to the naked eye. But no. The lady of the house went shopping and bought a pole lamp. Every workman on the job was in danger of being run out of town on a rail when the lady lit her pole lamp, because the walls and ceiling would look like nine miles of bad road.

For those readers who are young enough and fortunate enough to have no experience with pole lamps, they were 8-foot long, spring-loaded poles that could be wedged between the ceiling and the floor. Each pole lamp had sockets, or cans, that were mounted so as to be adjustable. The lady of the house would prop the pole lamp near a wall, usually alongside the sofa, and would adjust those infernal lamps or cans so they shone directly down the wall (two lamps) and across the ceiling (one lamp). With all surfaces of the room thus critically lighted, the lady would suddenly discover all the defects in the wall/ceiling. She could see every nail hole and every joint, and could count every stud in the wall. Complaint time!

I once answered a complaint call from a customer who had installed a pole lamp in her living room. She was agitated, to put it mildly, with the "lousy" job I had done on her walls. Why, you could count every joint in the wall! She demanded that I refinish the wall, and do it "right."

I demonstrated how to make light more critical or more flattering. When I turned the adjustable cans

and removed the direct sidelighting from the wall, it magically became flat and flawless. Look, I said, all you have to do is adjust the lights so the wall is not subjected to the worst possible critical lighting. But the lady was wise to my tricks, and protested that she wanted her lights *just* the way she had them. Who was I to tell her how to adjust her lamps?

I tried to make my point, that critical lighting is not mandatory and in fact not even intelligent. The light that the pole lamp reflected from the wall was unusable; you could not use it for reading or for any other purpose. What harm to turn the lamps slightly so the light did not fall so unflatteringly on the wall?

Again trying to mollify her, I did the light-in-the-garage trick. In the dark garage I rigged a 100-watt bulb so it would sidelight her expensive sedan's sheet metal. It looked not a bit better than my interior wallboard. So, I asked her, suppose you were going to show off your car, or offer it for sale. Would you remove the overhead garage light that makes the car look like a gleaming jewel, and instead sidelight it as I have done, so the light emphasizes every little wrinkle in the sheet metal? She thought the comparison ridiculous, but it is not. Common sense (often a most uncommon virtue) dictates that we use the lighting that is most flattering and most useful in our homes, and that we eliminate harsh sidelighting that makes our interior look like a candidate for urban renewal. After all, our goal is to make the house interior as attractive as possible. Why cast the results in unflattering or critical light?

The pole lamp is an extreme but by no means solitary example of bad light fixtures. Any light fixture that has a bare bulb at or near the surface of the ceiling or wall is another example of dumb lighting, and the examples are legion. Check out the porcelain lampholders that are often seen in basements, laundry rooms, hallways, or garage ceilings. They are used because they are cheap, and they are perfectly suitable for use in unfinished space. But just install a wallboard ceiling, tape and finish it, and apply paint, and that lampholder will directly sidelight the ceiling. The result is washboard city, another lesson in how to make a ceiling look as lousy as possible.

Other examples of lousy lighting include those $3.98 light fixtures that look like a Mason jar with a light bulb inside. These are commonly flush-mounted on entry, foyer, or hall ceilings, and the flush mounting puts the light bulb in perfect position to sidelight the ceiling. Remove those little dandies and replace them with a decent light, meaning an attractive fixture that either moves the bulbs lower or has cut glass globes that break up the light and end the critical view of the ceilings. I replaced the $2.98 hall fixtures in my own 1950-model house with $50 fixtures that actually reflect the light down toward the floor, so it is not only less critical but more useful. What a novel idea that is: useful, flattering light.

Another example of light fixtures that cause harm are the beauties that were installed in bedroom ceilings up until the 1960s. (About that time builders found an even less expensive alternative: *no* ceiling lights. The theory here is that it doesn't cost any more to skimp a little.) These light fixtures consist of two bulb sockets set at opposing angles, to hold two 60-watt bulbs flat against the ceiling. To avoid any possibility that some of the light will reflect downward and will actually become usable light, a dish-shaped fixture cover is held over the light bulbs via a small decorative retaining nut. Because these bare light bulbs lie almost flat against the ceiling, separated perhaps by a small aluminum reflector, there is always a warning to not use a bulb larger than X-watts in the fixture. The reason is that the extra heat from a larger bulb may ignite the framing and burn down your house. The best bet is to remove these flush-mounted fixtures and replace them with strip or downlighting, or install a ceiling fan that will provide some air movement as well as directing light downward where it might be usable.

Common light fixtures that create critical lighting include flush-mounted ceiling fixtures, unshaded lamps that directly sidelight the wall or ceiling, and porcelain lampholders that hold the bulb in an upright direction but still sidelight the surrounding surfaces. Light fixtures that direct light away from a ceiling or wall may include recessed lighting, strip lighting, downlighting, or suspended fixtures such as chandeliers. Ask your lighting dealer to help you select fixtures and lamps that are complimentary and project useful light.

SUNLIGHT

Artificial lighting is not the only offender when we are considering critical lighting. Large expanses of glass such as the wall-to-ceiling windows that have become popular in recent years can allow strong sunlight to enter the room, and the strong sunlight can have the same sidelighting effect as a light fixture that is set too close to the ceiling or wall. Because the light direction of incoming sunlight usually is down the length of a wall, sidelighting the surface, we strongly urge that all wallboard be installed so it is perpendicular, not parallel, to the framing (see Chapter 2, Installing Wallboard). Tests have shown that *joint banding*, or shadowing of the joints, is exaggerated when wallboard joints are parallel to the framing.

I once had a call-back on a wallboard job in which the ceilings were cathedral, soaring upwards from 8-foot height at the exterior walls to 14-foot height at the peak. The house faced a hill, and the wall facing the hill was all glass. To make matters worse, the hill on that winter day was snow-covered, and the snow reflected sunlight inside and onto the ceiling to an unbelievable degree. Because of the siting of the house, the incoming sunlight was at right angles to the ceiling joints, even though those joints were perpendicular to the framing. The total effect was that the joints showed so plainly that I was completely embarrassed to see the results of my own handiwork. But I was helpless to change the effect: the only solution was to hang draperies or shades to block the reflected light. The soaring ceiling of that room totalled over 800 square feet. One rule we have not discussed is that of all ceilings that look bad, larger ceilings look worse, because you can get a long-range perspective of a larger room ceiling.

As we stated, sunlight that streams in from all-glass walls or from skylights may project critical light across your walls or ceilings. For the sake of your interior furniture, carpets, and other furnishings, as well as your air-conditioning bills, use blinds, curtains, draperies, or awnings to block out direct sunlight.

USEFUL SHADOWS

With all our condemnation of critical sidelighting, it is worth noting that interior designers may also use sidelight and shadows to create dramatic and desirable styling results. Thick-butt asphalt shingles are advertised as casting a deep shadowline, thereby adding drama to the appearance of your roof and simulating expensive hand-split wood shakes. Embossed wall coverings are used to inject shadow and texture into the decorating scheme, and thick sculptured carpets add decorator interest to other planned effects (color, texture) to enhance the total room appeal. The ideal result is to control lighting so that light and shadow occur in a planned and controlled scheme, and do not occur as unwanted accidents that detract from the effect you are trying to create.

8

Soundproofing and Fireproofing

Before we start to build or remodel, we should ask ourselves just what functions we expect the partitions in our house to perform. Walls, ceilings, and floors create barriers between living areas, establish privacy curtains, and provide shelter from the elements. In most instances these are the performance requirements that we expect from the "envelopes" of our homes. But in some cases we may need to build or remodel the structure with additional demands in mind. We may want the walls, ceilings, or floors to provide other values such as enhanced soundproofing or fireproofing. In most cases the demands for soundproofing or fireproofing in residential buildings are not excessive, and the homeowner should be aware that it is relatively easy to build increased soundproofing or fireproofing into walls, ceilings, or floors that are under construction. In fact, it is not really difficult to increase the soundproofing or fireproofing value of existing walls, ceilings, or floors. A basic understanding of sound and fire control will let you do the job yourself or understand how a contractor would do the job for you. We will attempt here to give you a primer on how to control sound transmission and fire spread in a residential building.

The first step in understanding soundproofing or fireproofing procedures is to remember this basic fact: the amount of *mass* is the common and critical factor in solving both problems. The more dense the

building material, and the more mass or weight per square foot of the wall, ceiling, or floor, the greater the resistance to fire or to sound transfer. Because masonry is fire resistant as compared with other building materials, masonry is obviously a favored building material when fire may be a hazard. It is a known historic fact that, after Mrs. O'Leary's cow kicked over the lantern and started the Great Chicago Fire, the city fathers banned wood structures as commercial buildings when Chicago was rebuilt. But it is less recognized that even wood-framed buildings are more fire resistant if they are covered with a thicker wall, i.e., increased mass, of plaster or wallboard. The thicker the plaster or wallboard, or the more layers of wallboard added over the framing, the greater the fire rating of the wall or ceiling. The fire rating of a wall or ceiling is a measure of how long a fire can burn inside the room until the heat ignites the framing studs or joists. For example, ordinary $1/2$-inch thick wallboard, for years the standard thickness used for covering residential walls and ceilings, has a 45-minute fire rating. This means that it would take a fire burning inside a room 45 minutes before the wooden studs and joists would ignite within the wall and spread the fire into adjoining rooms.

Because of the greater fire danger that an attached garage represents, most building codes require that $5/8$-inch thick wallboard such as USG's Firecode be

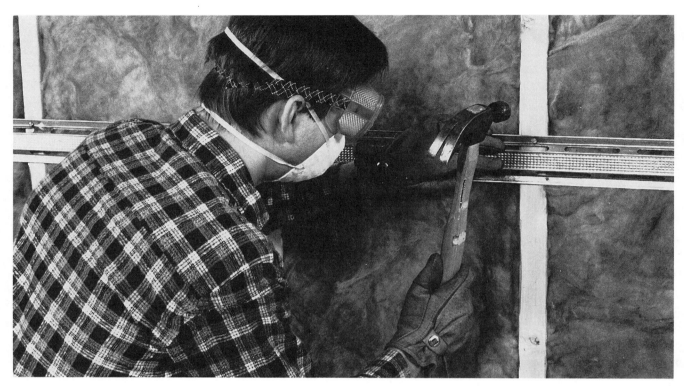

Fiberglass insulation, teamed with resilient steel channel, can reduce through-the-wall noises from a roar to a whisper. Wear eye goggles and mask when working with fiberglass. Photo courtesy of USG.

Closeup of resilient channel (center) shows how channel holds wallboard away from framing, reducing noise transmission through the partition. Photo courtesy of USG.

used on common walls or ceilings between the garage and the house interior. The thicker 5/8-inch thick wallboard has a 60-minute fire rating, meaning that a fire that originates in the garage will take one hour or 60 minutes to burn through the fire wall and spread into the house itself. This provides an additional 15-minute time advantage over the thinner 1/2-inch thick wallboard, so the greater fire rating obviously will provide the occupants of the house a greater warning time to notice the fire and abandon the house.

Controlling sound transfer also depends on the type of noise. For controlling airborne sounds, the remedy is to use caulk, weatherstripping, or insulation to block the paths through which air and sound can pass. But when sound is transferred through a partition via vibration or conduction, greater mass is also needed to provide added soundproofing in a wall or ceiling.

SOUNDPROOFING

As noted earlier, sound control methods depend on the source of the sound as well as the avenue it travels. Airborne sounds can be controlled with any method — caulking, weatherstripping, or insulating — that reduces air passage, either infiltration or exfiltration.

Another source of noise transfer is conduction. In this type of sound transfer, the sound wave strikes a surface, such as a wall, and sets it into vibration. The sound is transferred to the space on the opposite side of the wall via this vibration. To prevent this vibration, one can build greater mass into the wall. For example, a wall of solid masonry, or even of hollow concrete blocks, cannot be set into vibration by sound waves. These materials obviously stop sound transfer, because they cannot be set into vibration. But once you cut a door or window opening into that masonry wall, airborne noise will pass through the cracks around the opening.

Objectionable noise can originate within the house or can come from outside sources. For example, throughout the nation's cities, the government has built wooden sound barriers alongside the freeways to isolate car noises. Nationwide, the Federal Aviation Administration (FAA) is wrestling with airport noise control, as airports become busier and aircraft become noisier. The sources of noise pollution are many in our metropolitan areas: traffic, emergency vehicles, aircraft, and construction all contribute to our growing noise pollution.

I live at the end of a runway near the Minneapolis-St. Paul International Airport. Within two miles of my house interested agencies, with direction from Wyle Laboratories, an acoustical engineering firm, remodeled a "soundproof home" located at the end of an airport runway. Three levels of noise control have been included, with rooms showing a decibel improvement of 5dB, 10dB, and 15dB according to the number of materials added. So that those who tour the house can experience a contrast in noise levels, half the rooms in the house were left unaltered, with conventional construction. With this setup a person can walk from room to room and, by shutting doors, can experience the different levels of sound control provided. The sound control is quite remarkable in all three control zones.

The room with the 15dB noise reduction is designated the "quiet room." The remodelers actually built a "room within a room" in which a new ceiling and new walls were built inside, but independent of, existing ceiling and walls. In the ceiling above this room the insulation has been increased to R44. Ceiling air ducts have also been insulated, and a double wall (exterior walls only) system built. The door to the room is solid wood, not the usual hollow core type commonly used for interior doors today. The existing window was replaced with a set of two acoustic windows, set 4 inches apart. When a 727 jet flew over the house, a noise meter located in the room recorded a decibel level of 42dB, while a noise meter located outside the house shot up to 95.6dB.

In a walkout den at basement level the only change made was to replace an ordinary window with an acoustic model window. Acoustic windows are built with heavy glass, have air space of at least 2 inches between the two glass panes to ensure that the panes will not vibrate in unison, and have more efficient weatherstripping than ordinary windows. The window change alone provided a noise level reduction of 5dB.

Yet another room was fitted with a weatherstripped door of solid wood, ceiling insulation was increased to R44, and an extra layer of 5/8-inch thick wallboard was added to the ceiling and exterior walls. This produced an improvement in noise levels of 10dB. It can be seen that fairly inexpensive alterations can provide excellent sound control. In the 5dB and 10dB rooms you can still hear jet noises, but normal conversation can now be heard.

There is no final plan for this area, but present estimates are that the FAA will pay up to 80 percent of the cost of soundproofing those houses that are affected by excessive airport noises. Noise relief measures include the soundproofing mentioned, plus buyouts and purchase guarantees of the homes most affected. Wyle Laboratories is doing similar noise audits near airports across the nation. Cities where airport noise control is being studied, via federally funded programs, include Atlanta, Baltimore, Boston, Denver, Los Angeles, Pittsburgh, and Seattle.

What is a Decibel?

According to Wyle Laboratories' acoustic engineers, sound energy or noise is measured in units called decibels, abbreviated as dB. To halve the sound energy you do not have to reduce the decibels by half; you must reduce the total dB by only three dB to reduce the noise level. But because of the way we perceive sound, you must reduce the sound level by 10 dB to achieve a sense that the sound is only "half as loud." Rather than get caught up in the dB rating for various materials, it is perhaps easier for most of us to consider the sound transmission class

or STC of the total wall or ceiling. The rule to remember is that the higher the STC, the quieter the house.

Controlling Interior Noises

Ordinary 2 x 4 construction with 1/2-inch thick wallboard on both sides of the partition has a 32 STC. For a wall rated between 30 STC and 35 STC, loud speech can be heard through the wall of the adjoining room. If you improve the STC of the curtain wall to 42 STC, loud speech is heard as a murmur in the next room. If the two rooms are divided by a wall with 50 STC, loud speech cannot be heard from the next room.

As noted, 2 x 4 wall construction with 1/2-inch thick wallboard on both sides has a 32 STC. If you nail 1/2-inch thick SoundStop insulation board over the wallboard, on both sides of the wall, then glue another layer of 1/2-inch thick wallboard over the SoundStop board, you will have raised the STC to 46. SoundStop or other insulation board is available at your local lumber yard, or ask the dealer to order it for you. Or you can screw steel resilient channels over the existing wallboard, perpendicular to the framing and 24 inches on center, and screw a new layer of 5/8-inch thick wallboard onto the resilient channels on both sides of the wall. This approach will raise the sound rating of the partition to 46 STC. Resilient channel for wallboard is available at any wallboard dealer. Check the Yellow Pages of your phone book under "Dry Wall Contractors' Equipment & Supplies" to find a dealer.

If you are finishing off a basement ceiling and install 1/2-inch thick wallboard screwed over the floor/ceiling joists, you will get an STC rating of 32. But while you have access to the space between the joists, install fiberglass batt insulation between the joists, then nail or screw resilient steel channels to the bottom of the joists, 24 inches on center. Screw 5/8-inch thick wallboard to the resilient channels and finish and paint the wallboard. Install carpet over the floor above. You now have a 48 STC sound rating in your basement ceiling, or enough sound-

Sound transmission between floors of a building can be greatly reduced using fiberglass batt insulation and resilient channel. Note the resilient channel, installed first, supports unfaced fiberglass batt insulation. Photo courtesy of USG.

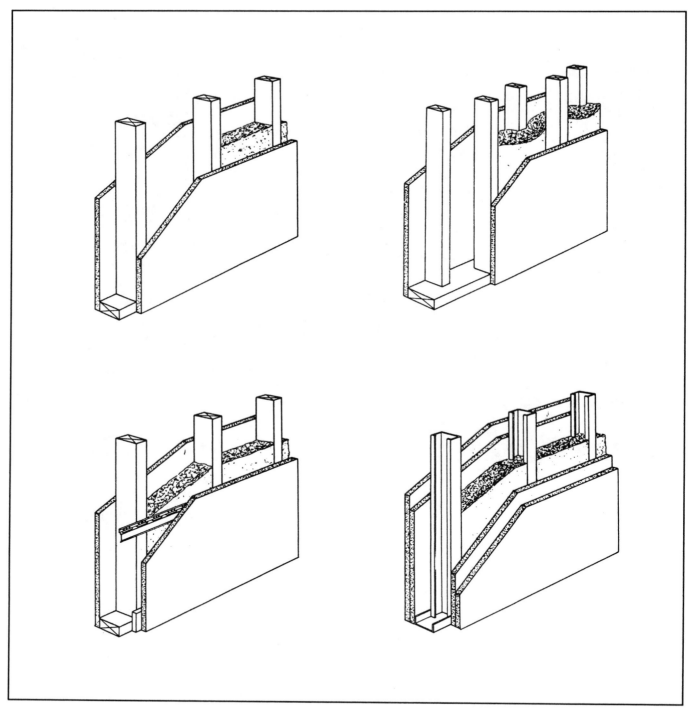

Illustrations demonstrate the sound reduction values of various building techniques. Top left, insulation; top right, staggered studs plus insulation; bottom left, resilient channel with insulation; and bottom right double layers of wallboard with insulation are all worthwhile for both sound and fire control. Illustration courtesy of USG.

proofing to stop loud conversations in one space from being heard in the room above or below. Additional soundproofing can be gained by finishing the wallboard with an acoustical spray finish.

If you are building or remodeling, remember that toilet noises can be embarrassing. You have heard those bathrooms in which flushing the toilet projects a Niagara-like sound into nearby rooms. Use batt insulation in any wall to help muffle sound transfer. This is especially important to do in any wall that contains plumbing pipes, because the insulation will muffle the gurgling sounds made by water supply or drain pipes. Also, stuff fiberglass insulation in the pipe holes through the studs to help prevent the pipes from banging against the studs.

Installing fiberglass insulation in any room partition can help reduce sound transfer through the wall. In addition to bathroom walls, the walls of the master bedroom, child's nursery, or a basement workshop (walls and ceilings) should also be considered for insulation and for noise control.

To stop airborne noise and seal cracks that can let noise filter through, caulk between the floor sheathing and sole plates at the bottom of the wall. Remove any electrical outlet covers and caulk or spackle any cracks between the plaster or wallboard and the electrical outlet, to stop noise transfer through the cracks. Use weatherstripping (for the bottom of the door) and door sweeps to block noise transfer through the cracks around the door frame. Hang solid wood doors for maximum sound resistance — they are much quieter than panel or hollow core doors. If you have a center hall floor plan, install doors at both ends of the hall to form a sound lock between bedrooms and the living area.

Think of sound control when buying interior furnishings. Any rough surface tends to absorb sound waves rather than reflecting them. For this reason, consider using acoustic spray texture on ceilings. Note that although any rough surface is better than a hard, smooth finish and is somewhat sound absorbent, you can buy special textures that have even better acoustical values than the standard spray texture found in most houses. Buy heavy-duty carpet and padding for floors, rather than using hard-surface wood, ceramic, or vinyl flooring. Draperies at windows not only help to stop sound bounce within the house, they help form a sound barrier to screen out outdoor noises.

Consider replacing older appliances that are both energy inefficient and noisy. New appliances may offer useful features that also will help you justify spending part of your budget on new appliances.

If you have really grown attached to your old shop tools, you may be reluctant to replace them. But it may be useful to take a tour through a dealer showroom and see what's new in tools. New features, quieter running, and added job capacity may entice you to give up the noisy old tools in favor of modern tools. You can also place rubber pads under the legs of stationary or benchtop tools to reduce vibration noises. Insulating walls and ceilings of the workshop and weatherstripping the door will also help control workshop noises.

Ceiling Noise Transfer

If your teenager insists on tap dancing or clogging in the upstairs bedroom, what can be done to stop the impact noise from coming through to your den below? It is important to understand that some soundproofing measures will stop noise transfer both ways and will benefit you when the teenager is dancing upstairs, as well as stopping your stereo from disturbing *her* rest if she decides to take a break. Examples of this two-way sound control include installing insulation batts between the ceiling joists and using a heavy pad and carpet (which is hard to tap dance on) on the floor of the teenager's room. Applying resilient channel and an extra layer of wallboard to the ceiling side of the floor also will be beneficial to both rooms.

By contrast, acoustical materials applied to the ceiling side of the room will stop noise from traveling upwards, through the ceiling and into the room

Framing in a second partition, completely separate from existing walls, can break up sound transmission and quiet house. Photo courtesy of Stanley Tools.

Here a workman screws on a layer of wallboard over batt insulation to stop noise transfer. Photo courtesy of USG.

Acoustic ceiling panels set in suspended metal grids can reduce noise transfer from a basement recreation room upwards into living quarters above. This means that the greatest sound barrier is on the acoustic side of the ceiling: the ceiling is most effective stopping noise from basement up, not from main floor down. Photo courtesy of Armstrong.

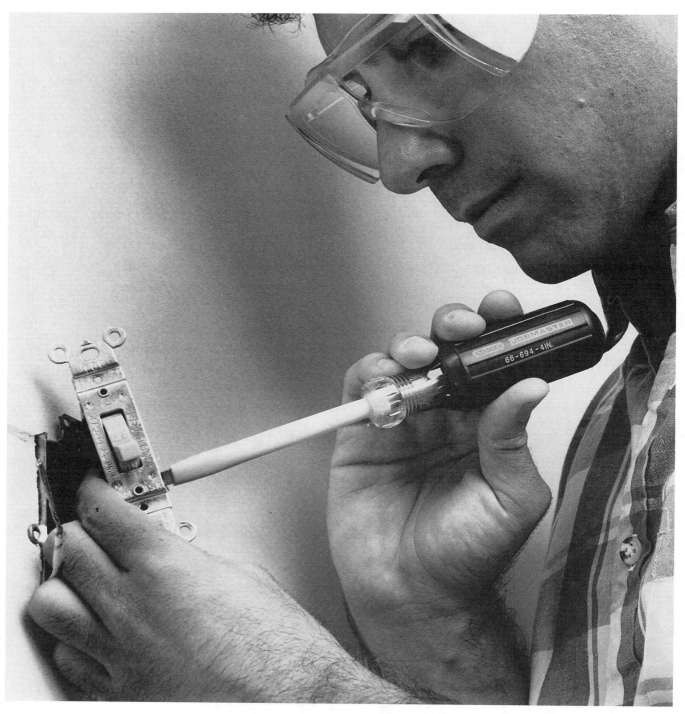

For best soundproofing, avoid openings for ducts and electrical outlets in walls or ceilings. Where openings cannot be avoided, use an acoustic sealant to seal the crack between the wallboard and the electrical outlet or duct. Photo courtesy of Stanley Tools.

above. Acoustical tile and spray acoustic textures are examples of this one-way soundproofing. But these sound-absorbent materials stop the noise only from the side to which they are applied: acoustic texture applied to your den ceiling won't have much effect on the impact sound of your teenager dancing on her bedroom floor above. Sound waves traveling downward through the ceiling will not be absorbed by the acoustic texture, so you want to install the sound treatment on the side the sound is coming *from*, where possible.

The best control for interior or family noises is always good manners. If the early bird clod in your family feels perfectly justified in disturbing the entire household by whistling through the morning breakfast or toilet activities, there is nothing short of disowning him or her that will let you enjoy your slumbers.

FIREPROOFING

Fireproofing is normally not a major concern in residential construction. Walls and ceilings of $1/2$-inch thick wallboard provide a 45-minute fire rating, considered by most authorities (and building codes nationally) to be sufficient for family safety. But you should understand the basics of building

fire resistance into walls and ceilings. Using $5/8$-inch thick Firecode in a basement utility room ceiling might provide precious extra time for family evacuation by containing a furnace-room fire from spreading to the living levels above.

Because of the danger of car fires, the main areas of concern for fire control in a single-family residence are any ceilings or walls that divide the house living space from an attached garage. Ordinarily this means installing $5/8$-inch thick Firecode 60 wallboard over the stud wall between the house and garage. If the garage is a "tuck under" model, meaning it joins the house not only at a common wall but has living space above the garage, ceiling wallboard also must be $5/8$-inch Firecode, to provide a 60-minute fire rating. All Firecode wallboard in garages should be taped to seal the joints and prevent fire from entering into the wall or ceiling cavity.

Traditional lath and plaster walls should have a fire rating of at least one hour, depending on the thickness of the plaster. Standard wallboard thickness for most residential walls is $1/2$ inch, for a fire rating of 45 minutes. Remember, each extra layer of wallboard adds another increment of time equal to the first: $1/2$ inch for an additional 45 minutes, $5/8$ inch for an additional 60 minutes.

9
Wall Fasteners and Hanging Pictures

A common problem for homeowners is where and how to hang pictures, mirrors, or draperies (hardware) on a wall. Special fasteners are available that permit you to hang lightweight objects at almost any location of your choice. Before selecting a fastener or hanger, consider the weight of the object you will be hanging and check the label directions on the fastener package to be sure the fastener or hanger is approved for bearing that amount of weight.

For hanging heavy objects such as mirrors, the best choice for maximum support is to drive the fastener(s) into wall studs or ceiling joists. The only question then is how to locate the stud or joist concealed in the wall or ceiling. In this chapter we will discuss how to find the wood framing members concealed in the wall or ceiling, and how to overcome special problems that can arise when working with fasteners and wall hangers.

HOW TO LOCATE STUDS AND JOISTS

Basic to framing of modern houses is the layout, or positioning of studs, joists, and/or trusses at predetermined intervals. Although the rules for framing are not hard and fast, the age of your house may provide clues to the framing interval. In houses that are more than twenty years old, most framing members are set at intervals of 16 inches, center-to-center, or 16 in. o.c. In houses built in the past twenty years, the ceiling joists used in "stick build-ing" often were replaced by roof trusses, set 24 inches o.c. Wall framing under the roof trusses may be either 16 or 24 inches on center. The point is, if you know the framing interval of your house, once you have found one stud or joist, it is easy to measure across the wall or ceiling and find the rest of the framing members at those intervals.

Another method of finding wall studs is to check the nail pattern in the baseboard trim. The trim carpenter nails the trim on by driving nails into the wall studs, because nails driven into the wood flooring or carpet underlayment would interfere with the seasonal expansion and contraction of the wood flooring or underlayment. If the finishing of the trim was done professionally, the nail holes in the baseboard trim may be hard to find, because they are concealed with wood putty. But by close examination or by using a magnetic stud finder you will find the baseboard nails, and once you have found them you need only use a plumb bob or carpenter's square to line up the studs above.

Another way to locate studs in a wall is to remember that electrical outlets are usually nailed directly to the side of a stud (*usually*, because electrical outlets are sometimes supported by brackets so they hang between studs). If you remove the outlet cover and peer into the outlet box you may be able to see a nailhead on one side of the box. If there is a crack in the plaster or wallboard, around the perimeter of the outlet box, use a plastic ruler to probe alongside the

Inexpensive magnetic stud finder is a plastic box containing a magnetic arrow set on a swivel. As the unit is passed over nails in wall studs or plaster lath, the magnetic arrow points to the stud. Photo by the author.

Electronic stud finder measures the density of the wall, sensing increased density at stud or joist locations. Electronic stud finders cost about $20. Photo by the author.

outlet box and find the stud. Turn off the electric power to that outlet before probing and never use a metal object as a probe, because the metal probe will conduct electricity. When you have located the stud and have determined the stud interval — either 16 inches o.c. or 24 inches o.c. — measure with a ruler to find studs on either side of the electrical outlet box.

USING A STUD FINDER

Another way to find framing is to use a stud finder. For a couple of dollars you can buy a simple magnetic stud finder. The magnetic stud finder has a magnetic arrow set on a rotating shaft, inside a small plastic cover. As you move the stud finder over the surface of the wall, the magnet will sense any nails in the wall, such as lath nails under plaster or wallboard nails or screws. When the magnet senses metal it will swing into position, perpendicular to the wall, and you will know there is a stud at that location.

Another type of stud finder is the electronic model. The electronic stud finder locates studs by measuring the increased wall density over studs or joists. When these were first introduced I was prepared to dismiss these electronic stud finders as gimmicks. Upon investigation and trial I found them to be very accurate, and I would suggest that any homeowner buy one to save the frustration and damage done by "fishing" for studs on a trial-and-error basis. One word of warning, however: I had to practice with the electronic stud finder a bit before I learned to read it, or to understand what I was seeing, so it may take a bit of practice to get the hang of it. My problem may have been that I did not trust the accuracy of the device until I positioned it over a known stud location and the stud finder confirmed what I already knew to be true.

HANGING OBJECTS ON WALLBOARD

Hanging objects can be especially difficult when the wall material is wallboard, because the soft plaster core of wallboard will not support a fastener such as a nail or screw. You must either locate a wall stud (or a ceiling joist, if you are hanging some object from the ceiling) or use a specially-designed fastener such as a toggle bolt or a "Molly" screw to hang any object from wallboard. These fasteners can be very effective and can support a surprising amount of weight. As mentioned earlier, however, it is very important to check the hanger package to be sure the hanger you are buying will hold the weight of the object you are hanging.

One such hanger that I have used is the Wall Grabber. The Wall Grabber is modeled upon automotive fasteners and has a shaft down the center of the fastener, separating two spring steel legs. The spring steel legs can be driven with a hammer into soft materials such as wallboard. A screw is turned in the threaded shaft, and as the screw is turned the steel legs spread and lock the hanger into place on the backside of the wallboard. The plus is that, unlike the Molly-type fastener, which must be drilled out for removal, the screw can be withdrawn from the Wall Grabber, and the spring steel legs come back together. You can then grasp the shaft of the fastener with pliers and simply pull the hanger out of the wallboard. The only damage to be patched after the hanger is withdrawn is a small, 1/2-inch long slit in the wallboard.

Other Wall Grabbers can be used in hollow core doors or in concrete walls. You cannot drive the hangers into these materials. Starter holes must be drilled first and the hanger inserted.

One thing to remember when you are remodeling: draperies are heavy, and there invariably is no wood to support the drapery hardware at window corners. Before installing wallboard, cut scraps of joists and nail them between the window header and the nearest stud, at the top of the window or at normal drapery height. Then, when you get ready to hang the draperies, you will have solid wood to which you can screw the drapery hardware. As simple as this sounds, I have seen very few carpenters who anticipated this frustrating problem by installing backing or nailers at drapery height.

HANGING OBJECTS ON PLASTER

Hanging objects on plaster walls or ceilings can be much easier than hanging them on wallboard, especially if the plaster has a base of wood lath. Plaster alone is dense enough to support small nails or screws, which in turn will support small pictures or photos on the wall. The 1/4-inch thick wood lath will itself support heavy weights and can be used to hold most wall loads you will want to hang. Also, the laths are applied over the entire wall, separated only by a gap about 1/4-inch wide that lets the plaster droop or "key" behind the lath. If you drive a hanger or fastener into the gap between the laths, you need only raise or lower the hanger by about 3/4-inch and you will find a wood lath to support your hanging.

One common mistake is to drive a nail into a plastered wall, thus cracking the plaster. Because plaster is brittle, it will crack easily when it is subjected to an impact tool such as a swung hammer. Also, the wood lath beneath the plaster coat is limber and "springy." If you drive a nail through the plaster and into the wood lath, the nail point may not penetrate into the limber wood, but may instead cause it to flex and vibrate as the nail is struck. The result will be either a crack in the surface plaster or a loss of key strength when the wood lath is flexed and the supporting keys break free from the plaster. Rather than trying to drive a nail into plaster, use a drill to predrill a hole for the fastener or hanger. Using the drill will serve a double purpose. First, watch the drill bit as it goes through the plaster: if you see sawdust coming out of the hole as the bit turns, so you know you have hit wood — the stud or wood lath. And second, you will avoid impact damage to the plaster surface or to the hidden plaster keys within the walls. Always use a drill and predrill a hole when installing hangers or any fastener in plaster.

Plaster that is sound also is dense enough to support plastic screw anchors. The plastic anchors are available in a variety of sizes, depending on the size screw needed for the job at hand. As a screw is driven into a plastic anchor, the anchor expands and the fluted sides of the anchor grip against the plaster. Plastic anchors can be used not only in plaster, but in wallboard, concrete, and ceramic tile to support hangers or other objects such as shower door frames or towel racks. Be sure to use the right size drill bit when predrilling holes for plastic anchors. Holes that are oversized will not provide as good support as will the proper size hole, and the anchor may loosen or fail.

If you are hanging a heavy object such as a house plant from the ceiling, by all means drive the hanger into solid wood. Any weight that is hung from the ceiling hangs in a position of direct withdrawal to the fastener, meaning that the weight is acting in line to the direction in which the fastener was driven, and thus the direction of easiest withdrawal.

If you absolutely must hang the weighty object in one exact position, and cannot move it over a bit so it is directly underneath a joist, you should use a toggle bolt as the hanger of second choice. After being inserted into the predrilled hole, the toggle on the bolt spreads open. The spread legs of the toggle will distribute the weight over a larger area, and thus will provide greater support than an ordinary nail or screw fastener could provide.

Be wary of hanging any object on the adhesive-backed hangers that are offered today. Moisture from the bath or from cooking and any wax on the surface to which it is attached may interfere with the adhesive backing, and the hanger may fail. I have never had any success at all with adhesive-backed hangers, and I would be reluctant to hang anything (breakable) of value from such a hanger.

Use a hammer to drive wall hangers such as the Wall Grabber into wallboard. The sharp point on the anchor penetrates wallboard with little damage. Photo by the author.

Use a screwdriver to drive a screw into the Grabber anchor. The screw spreads the spring-steel legs of the anchor, locking the anchor in place. Photo by the author.

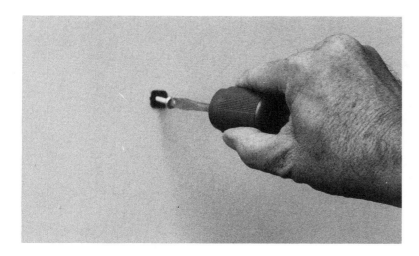

To remove the Grabber, remove the screw, then use pliers to pull the anchor out of the wallboard. The removed anchor leaves only a small slot in the wallboard to be repaired. Photo by the author.

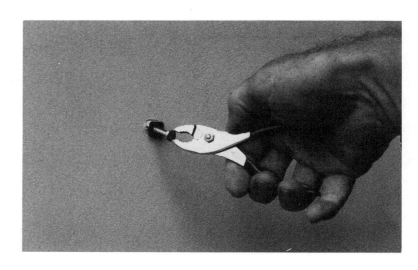

10
Paneling and Moldings

The economic depression of the 1930s was followed by the civilian materials shortages of World War II, so little new housing was built in the U.S. for a period of twenty years (1928 to 1948). After 1945, as young people returned from military duties and began to marry and form new families, there was a great housing shortage, and young people began to buy and renovate older housing. Coincidental with this boom in housing renovation was the development of a new building material: plywood paneling.

Wall paneling was nothing new in those post-war years: solid wood walls of oak, walnut, mahogany, and other attractive wood species had been included in the homes of the rich for many decades. But inexpensive plywood paneling, glued together using backer plies of inexpensive softwood and a face or finish layer of oak or mahogany, put the wood look within the budget of the middle class.

Combine the two developments — a great increase in home remodeling plus the development of plywood paneling — and it was inevitable that the young couples would decide that cover-up, not repair of old cracked plaster walls, was the answer. People began to buy cartop carriers to cart home acres of cheap plywood paneling. The use of cheap paneling, usually mahogany, to cover old walls was rampant. Beautiful older homes were thus "converted" to the paneled look, and the results were uniformly disastrous. This approach to remodeling was called "remuddling" by Clem Labine of the *Old House Journal* magazine. Using plywood paneling became a no-no, paneling soon lost popularity, and

plywood paneling sales plummeted. Restorers of old houses began ripping off the cheap paneling and repairing the old plaster to return the house to its original condition. So who was right: those who chose paneling or those who removed and discarded it?

The drawbacks of paneling include an end to variety in decorating choice. Once the paneling is installed you can no longer change the paint color or decide to decorate with wall covering. You should choose paneling carefully, because once it is installed you must learn to love it. Keep in mind too that cheap materials rarely show quality: cheap paint, cheap paneling, and cheap wall covering just plain look cheap. So if you decide to install paneling, keep in mind Branson's Law #1: You don't always get what you pay for but you *never* get more than you pay for. If you are sure you want paneling, spend enough money to buy a quality product that will be durable and will continue to show quality.

The pluses of using plywood paneling include the fact that most Americans share a love affair with wood. From early colonial times of solid-wood timber or log houses, wood has been an available, attractive, and affordable building material. If properly executed using a quality wood species such as oak, pecky cypress, or mahogany, wood paneling will yield a warmth and charm that few other interior building materials can duplicate.

Other desirable features of wood paneling include ease of cleaning and lack of maintenance, plus a durable surface that will absorb a lot of family activity and wear and tear. Used in a recreation room and properly reinforced with gypsum backerboard, wood paneling will withstand the impact of a badly aimed pool cue or the handlebars of a toddler's tricycle. If you choose prefinished plywood paneling, you will not only "nail the finish on" with the paneling, you will avoid frequent redecorating expense and labor. These pluses make wood paneling a choice worth considering when you are remodeling or building a room addition.

Another point to consider when choosing plywood paneling is the suitability of the material for any particular room. Wood paneling is commonly used as a wall finish in recreation rooms, dens, libraries, halls, stairways, and home offices. It is also used as wainscoting, meaning a wood covering for walls that is usually applied either 48 inches or 32 inches up from the floor. This lower-wall covering is used both for decorative purposes and to protect plaster or wallboard from damage. It is most often installed where the lower wall is subject to impact or traffic damage, such as in a hallway. The 32-inch height is also called "chair rail" height, or the level at which most chair backs might strike the walls of a dining room or kitchen breakfast nook.

Wood paneling is normally not advisable for use in the bath or in any area that is subject to moisture and requires frequent cleaning. If you are building a spa-type bathroom with a hot tub or whirlpool tub, and would like the ambience of a wood interior, do not use plywood paneling, which might delaminate or come apart between plies. Instead, use solid wood tongue-and-groove boards such as interior redwood or cedar, coated with polyurethane finish, for maximum wood durability in a bathroom.

INSTALLING PANELING

It is generally advisable to avoid using cheaper grades of paneling. Cheap hardboard panels with printed vinyl coverings that simulate wood grain are subject to warping and surface damage from impact. If you nick that paper-thin vinyl covering you will expose a dark brown or black hardboard core that is unattractive and difficult to repair. Also, the hardboard panels are difficult to plane or cut, making installation more difficult. Spend a few bucks extra and buy an all-wood product that has a real wood top or face ply.

If you are installing solid wood tongue-and-groove planks, 3/4 inch thick, you can simply install intermediate 2 x 4 nailers between the wall studs. Install the nailers at 24-inch intervals between the top and sole or bottom wall plates. This step ensures that you have something to nail the vertical boards to when you are between studs. Then you can toenail all vertical boards on the tongue side, at the top and bottom 2 x 4 wall plates and at 24-inch intervals from top to bottom. Because you nail the boards through the tongue side, the nails are all concealed and there are no nail heads to treat.

When installing plank or board paneling, you should buy from a dealer who has humidity-controlled storage space, so the boards will be straight and will not warp or shrink when installed. When you bring the wood planks home, stack them in the work space and let them sit for several days to "acclimate" or to reach parity of temperature and humidity with the space where they will be installed. The goal here is to let the wood planks lose moisture or shrink as much as they will before they are installed. Wood that shrinks after being installed will leave gaps or cracks at the joints, may warp or crack, and may experience finish damage from moisture. That is why one lets wood materials acclimate in the work space before nailing them in place.

INSTALLING PLYWOOD PANELING

Tools you will need to install paneling include: a hand saw, a circular saw with a plywood blade, a saber saw or keyhole saw, a carpenter's hammer and color-coded panel nails, contact or panel adhesives, caulk gun (for panel adhesive) or paint roller (for contact adhesives), a small wood plane, a

Irregular corners in paneled walls can be matched by scribing with a compass. Set the panel to be cut so it is plumb, 1 inch away from the corner, then use the compass to scribe as shown. As you move the compass along the edge, the sharp leg of the compass will move to match the corner; the pencil leg will record the actual contour of the corner. To match the corner, use a saber saw to cut carefully along the scribed line. Photo courtesy of Plywood Paneling Council.

Set any electrical outlets so their faces match the surface level of the paneling. Shim the screws of the outlets if necessary to move outlets outward. Install outlet box covers. Photo courtesy of Plywood Paneling Council.

prybar or lifter to lift the panels into place against the ceiling, a carpenter's pencil, sandpaper to smooth cut edges, a square, a level, a chalk box, and protective eye goggles.

Most plywood paneling is only 1/4 inch thick, give or take a sixteenth of an inch, and is not of itself rigid enough to be installed directly over framing. Instead, plywood paneling should be installed over a solid base of gypsum backerboard. The most commonly used backer for paneling is 3/8-inch thick wallboard. To make the panels even more rigid and resistant to damage, you should use panel adhesive or contact adhesive to secure the panels to the backerboard. When installing the panels, lay out the project so that joints in the paneling do not fall directly atop the joints in the wallboard backer panels.

In addition to adhesive application, there are paneling nails available that have painted heads, color-coded to match the paneling. Use color-coded nails where nailing is necessary, but use panel adhesives where possible to ensure a solid wall and to avoid having nail holes in the face of the panels.

Before starting actual panel application, arrange the panels around the room and check the wood grain pattern from panel to panel. Panels that have a wild grain pattern should be positioned together, on the same wall(s); panels with lesser pattern markings should also be positioned together, so there is no wide pattern variation from panel to panel. When you are pleased with the pattern it is time to begin installing the panels.

The face ply or veneer on plywood is subject to splintering when being cut, and the splintering is worse as the teeth of the saw blade exit the material. For this reason you should always place the panel so the teeth of the saw cut into the face ply first. For example, a circular saw blade cuts counterclockwise, entering the bottom side of the material first and cutting upwards, so you should place the panel face down when you are cutting it with a circular saw. If you are cutting the panel with a table saw, the

blade enters the top ply first and cuts downward. You should place the panels face up when cutting with a table saw. A hand saw cuts on the downstroke, so you should position the panel face up on the sawhorse when you are cutting with a hand saw to minimize splintering of the face ply.

Because 4 foot x 8 foot plywood panels are large and flexible, be sure to supply plenty of panel support before starting the cut. Four to six 2 x 4s, 8 feet long, equally spaced apart and laid between two sawhorses, will provide support to keep the panel or the cutoff panel section from falling while being cut.

Another help in avoiding splintering the face ply of the panel is to use a special plywood saw blade. Circular or table saw blades with many small teeth are available for cutting plywood, and it is really important to use this special blade when cutting prefinished paneling. Don't try to make do with a combination saw blade, because it cannot produce as fine a cut as a paneling blade.

Plywood paneling is dried and stabilized against shrinking as it comes to the consumer, because it is manufactured under highly controlled temperature and humidity conditions. Still, every building material has some expansion factor, so it is wise to paint a strip of stain on the backerboard at all joint locations. This way, if the panels shrink slightly and let a narrow strip of the backerboard become visible, you will not have a white streak peeking through down the center of the joint. One note: The stain used on the backerboard should match the finish of the paneling — not necessarily a "dark" stain as is often recommended, but a stain to match the paneling.

Measure and cut carefully to ensure a professional look to the finished job. Use a saber saw to cut holes for electrical outlets or for heating ducts. To avoid overcutting at inside corners, such as a notch in the paneling to fit over a window, make the cut to within an inch of the corner, using the circular saw. Then use a hand saw to finish the cut square to the corner.

Cut the panel to fit and set it in place to be sure all your cuts are right. After test-fitting the panel, use a caulking gun to apply panel adhesive from a caulk tube to the back of the panel. If you are using a contact-type adhesive, use a paint roller to apply the contact adhesive to both the wall backerboard and the back side of the panel. Then set the panel in place and use color-coded nails to tack it lightly to the top wall 2 x 4 plate. Then press the panel in place against the backerboard, being sure to make a matching fit at any joints. If you are using panel adhesive, press the panel against the wall to make contact with the adhesive, then pull the bottom of the panel slightly away from the wall so air can reach the panel adhesive. Then press the panel in place for its final positioning.

If you are using contact adhesive, just tack-nail the top of the panel to the top wall 2 x 4 plate to hold it in place until the contact adhesive takes hold. Use a rubber mallet and a 2 x 4 block wrapped in adhesive tape to strike the surface of the panel repeatedly and to ensure total contact with the backerboard. Then move your hand over the surface of the panel and slap the panel with the flat of your hand to be sure there are no loose spots where there is no bond between the panel and the backerboard. When you are satisfied that the panel is in full contact use a few color-coded panel nails to hold the panel in place until the adhesive sets. You can place the panel nails in the top and bottom 2 x 4 plates where they will be covered by molding.

Because we promised to give you only the best way to do these projects, and because the best way to apply paneling is to use panel adhesives, we have not talked about nailing on the paneling. Nailing does not afford the total panel support that one gets using panel adhesives, and nailing obviously will leave nailholes that must be puttied. If you do decide to nail on paneling, use color-coded nails and set them in panel grooves or in a spot where there is wood grain, to help conceal the nails. Or drive the nails at the top and bottom edges of the panels where trim or molding will cover the nails.

MOLDINGS

As with wall paneling, moldings were once considered a major decorative material in house interiors. Moldings were used to vary the decorative effect and to make an individual statement about the house. But that was in the days of low labor and material costs. In post-World War II housing, simplicity equalled low cost, and economy was the name of the game. The beautiful cove and crown moldings that once set off the living room ceiling gave way to a simple taped and painted corner. In recent years, however, the baby boomer generation has rediscovered decorative moldings, and new homes, especially those in upper income brackets, now boast fancy decorative moldings that rival the splendor of the old Victorian homes of yesteryear.

Moldings are generally described as being narrow wood or plastic members that are used for decorative purposes and/or to conceal the cracks where one building material meets another. Moldings are available in various shapes, depending on the use to which they will be put. Base and shoe moldings cover the crack where the floor meets the wall. L-shaped cap moldings are used to finish off the crack where wainscoting meets the wall. Crown or complicated cove moldings are used for decorative purposes or to cover the corner where the ceiling meets the walls.

Some moldings are used for decorative purposes only. For example, a number of molding shapes may be combined to form a fancy crown molding at a living room ceiling/wall juncture. In older houses, three or four pieces of molding, called three- or four-step molding, may be combined to form a base molding at the floor/wall juncture. Or moldings may be applied to walls, ceilings, doors, or furniture to make decorative designs and to break up the plain, flat surfaces.

One common source of damage to plaster or wallboard walls is from chair backs that are bumped against walls when diners push their chairs back after a meal. One flat decorative molding, called a

Remove any window trim and carefully cut out the opening for the window(s). Use colored paneling nails or panel adhesive to attach the paneling to the wall. Photo courtesy of Plywood Paneling Council.

Striking effects can be achieved using decorative panels on upper portion of the room, wood grain paneling to wainscot height (usually either 32 inches, shown, or 48 inches from floor), and chair rail and cove moldings at paneling and ceiling junctures respectively. Photo courtesy of Plywood Paneling Council.

chair rail, can be installed 32 inches (chair height) up from the floor to serve as a barrier to prevent damage to walls. But in addition to protecting walls from being bumped by chairs, the chair rails can serve a decorative function, separating wall covering on the upper portion of the wall from paint used to cover the lower one-half or one-third of the wall. By painting below the chair rail, you can also avoid getting wall covering damaged or dirty when mopping or cleaning floors. Nor is the use of chair rail molding limited to kitchens or dining areas. Take a master bedroom and chalk a line 32 inches above the floor. Install chair rail along the line on all walls. Paint the chair rail your choice of colors, or stain and varnish it to match the window and other trim in the room. Then paint the upper two-thirds of the walls in the color of your choice, with the lower one-third, the portion below the chair rail, white or some lighter color. You can make an amazing difference in a room by installing chair rail. Or apply an attractive wall covering above the chair rail, and use a complementary or contrasting paint color below the chair rail. The change one can make in a room is amazing, all for the cost of the chair rail, some paper, and paint. This low-cost decorating technique can transform a room. To check the effect for yourself, install chair rail in a small bedroom, or check the open houses in upper-bracket areas next weekend. You're sure to see some interesting treatments done with chair rail and other moldings.

Installing Moldings

Moldings are easy to work with and easy for the do-it-yourselfer to apply. Tools you will need include a carpenter's hammer, a nail set, a back saw, and an accurate miter box. (Don't try to use the simple wooden miter boxes because they are not accurate enough: if you don't own a good miter box, rent one.) You will also need sharp pencils (the emphasis is on *sharp*, because you need to mark moldings with a fine pencil point to make accurate cuts), a coping saw, a measuring tape, a razor knife, and some sandpaper.

Cutting the joints for moldings is simple. In most cases the cut involves positioning the molding in the miter box in the same attitude or position it will have when it is fitted in place. The only molding that is difficult to cut is the sprung cove molding used at wall/ceiling corners. Sprung cove molding is so-called because the back of the molding is *sprung* away from the wall at the apex of the corner. This sprung feature, or hollow curve at the center back of the molding, ensures that the molding will fit tightly in place on the edges, against the wall and ceiling lines, regardless of whether the plastered corner is square or not. In order to cut sprung cove molding, you must place the molding upside down in the miter box so that the ceiling side of the cove molding is against the bottom or base of the miter box and the wall side of the molding is set against the vertical back of the miter box. If that sounds confusing, remember you must set the molding so that its position or attitude is the same when it is sitting in the miter box as it will be on the wall/ceiling, meaning you cannot cut the molding in one position and install it in yet another position. To make it easier, we will show you how to cut a filler block you can use to hold the crown molding in position in the miter box (see on page 111).

Other joints in moldings are easy to make. Simple picture frame molding should be laid flat in the miter box and cut at a 45-degree angle at each corner. The same is true of window and door casing trim. One tip for cutting casing or door trim: when cutting the casing molding for a door, select a piece of molding that is a bit longer than the distance from the floor up to the top of the top door casing. Then cut a 45-degree miter on the top end of the side molding. Now turn the molding upside down, with the high point of the miter resting on the floor, but being careful not to bang the tip of the miter cut. Now, at the top end, mark the casing piece for length, and cut a square end on the casing. When you turn the piece over you will have a tight fit at both the top or mitered end and at the floor or square end. If you try to cut the casing to the exact length, set it on the floor and try to cut the miter end, you will often have a gap either at the miter end at top or between the bottom end of the casing and the floor.

Base molding is mitered sitting upright in the miter box, with the flat side of the base molding sitting against the vertical rear base of the miter box. Cut base shoe joints at 45-degree miters, called scarf joints. The miter cut where base shoe meets permits the base shoe to shrink without showing an open joint or crack, as a 90-degree square cut would do.

As mentioned, cut base moldings by setting them upright against the back vertical base of the miter box, so it sits against the back base of the box just as it will sit against the wall when installed. For outside corners, cut 45-degree miters on both of the meeting ends of base molding. Match the two mitered ends together where they meet at the outside corner.

Because inside corners of a room are never a true square or 90-degree angle, the directions for cutting inside corners on base moldings are a bit more complicated than just making simple 45-degree miter cuts. For cutting inside corners on base moldings, first cut a square end on one piece of molding and nail it in place with the square end tight against the corner. Then, assuming that this first piece of base molding is installed against a wall to your left (the directions for the cut will be the opposite if the base molding to be joined is to your right, i.e., make a left-hand miter cut), cut a 45-degree right-hand miter on the end of another piece of base molding. Now use the pencil tip to darken the edge of the miter cut, to define the profile of the molding. Then, using a coping saw, cut away the mitered end along the profile edge of the molding. The resulting coped cut will fit tightly against the base and will result in a tight joint, whether the corner is actually square — a true 90-degree angle — or not.

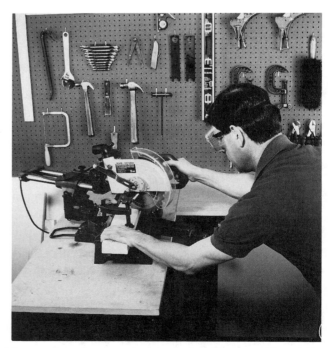

The compound power miter saw is the ultimate tool for working with moldings. Use the saw for crosscuts, miters, bevels, and compound cuts. Power miter saws are extremely accurate, yield perfect miter cuts. Photos courtesy of Sears.

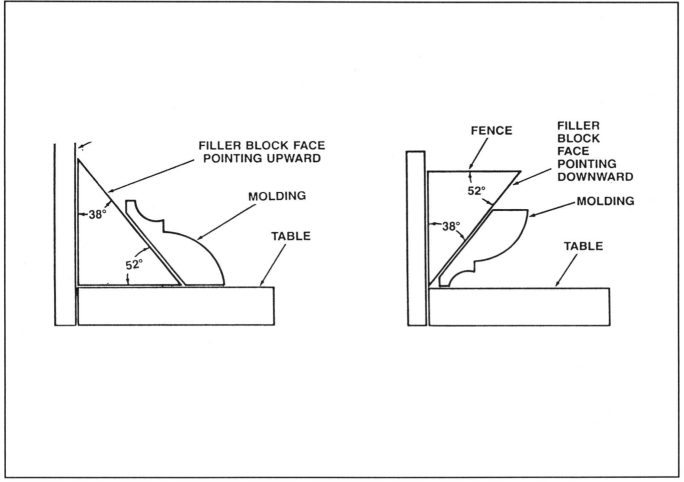

Position the filler block in the miter box either face upward or face downward. To cut corner miter in crown molding, position molding in miter box as shown. Courtesy of Sears.

You can become proficient in working with moldings by simply practicing the various miter cuts on scrap moldings. With a little practice, you will be making molding joints to be proud of. Do not forget our basic advice, however. You need a sharp pencil to make a sharp cut line, and you need an accurate miter box that will cut true to frame pictures or to install trim or decorative moldings.

To fasten moldings in place you can use adhesives or use the smallest finish (headless) nail that will do the job. Note that base molding should be nailed to the wall sole or bottom plate, or to the wall's 2 x 4 studs, not to the flooring. The base molding should sit atop the flooring, not joined to it by nails, so that the flooring material can expand and contract as the seasons and humidity change. Otherwise, the nailed flooring will buckle or the base molding will warp or split when the flooring moves. At miter joints in picture framing or in door or window casing, dry-fit the miter joints to be sure they are a close fit. Then spread carpenter's white glue on the miter cuts and joint them together. Nail the miters together through predrilled, angled nail holes that will pull the miter joint tightly together. When the glue sets, the miter joint should never open up again, and you will always have a tight miter joint.

11
Working with Wall Covering

Wall coverings are often still referred to as "wallpaper" although most modern coverings are made of vinyl, not paper. The history of wall coverings began when wealthy people could afford to cover their drafty wooden walls with leather, to stop air infiltration in winter. As old-style construction was abandoned and interior walls and ceilings were covered and cracks sealed with plaster, the problem of drafts was eliminated, so wall coverings became less necessary for weatherization. Instead, the wealthy could afford to hire artists to paint colorful and decorative murals on the plastered walls. But with the development of paper and printing presses, wall coverings became an inexpensive way to improve the interior of the home, and the middle class could imitate the murals of the rich by hanging decorative wall coverings. Wall coverings were used not only for their decorative versatility but for their ability to cover up problem walls and ceilings. Wall coverings have enjoyed varying levels of popularity for decades.

Following World War II, there was an urgent need to produce thousands of units of affordable housing, and speed of construction was the only virtue. Along with rounded arches, coved ceilings, paneled walls, and other amenities, wall coverings were abandoned in favor of economical flat paint. In the past few years, as two wage-earner families have become common, increasing the disposable in-comes of most households, the low-budget flat paint interiors of the past decades have yielded to an increasing consumer interest in the decorating flexibility offered by the many wall covering styles available.

WALL COVERING TYPES

There are thousands of wall coverings to choose from, so one must go through a process of elimination to narrow the field to a few final options. A brief comparison of the basic wall coverings offered may aid you in choosing the right one for your particular application. Also, consider that some wall coverings are easy for the amateur to install, and some are so difficult to work with that one should consider having them hung by an expert installer. Be aware too that it is easier to hang wall covering on walls than on ceilings; that rooms with large walls and few obstructions are easier to hang than a small bathroom with many nooks and crannies to cut and fit around. Also, a common complaint with wall coverings in the past was the difficulty of removing them. Steaming and other removal methods were hard, messy work. To avoid the mess of wall covering removal, choose a covering that is *strippable*. Consider the degree of difficulty for hanging the wall covering of your choice, and how "cut up" the room is that will be hung, before deciding whether to hang the covering yourself or hire a pro to do the job.

Following is a brief review of the types of wall coverings, their characteristics and difficulty of installation, to help guide you in your selection.

- **Vinyl** wall coverings are available prepasted, with the adhesive already on the back, and this ease of application makes them the most popular choice with do-it-yourselfers. The vinyl wall coverings may have a thin paper backing that makes them *peelable* when you want to remove them. This means you can peel the surface vinyl away from the paper backing, then soak the paper loose from the wall or ceiling to complete the removal process. Or the coverings may be *strippable*, meaning that a release-type adhesive is used that makes the covering easy to remove with little residue left on the wall or ceiling.

- **Fabric or woven textile** wall coverings can have the appearance of denim, linen, or other cloth material. Fabrics have no pattern to match, which makes them easy for the amateur to install. Fabric may be difficult to clean, so install such wall coverings in low-traffic areas.

- **Foils** have a surface coating of metallic film, which makes them difficult to install. The high light-reflective qualities of the foils makes them emphasize any surface defects, so you should prepare the wall or ceiling very carefully to receive any foil wall covering. Be very careful when handling foils around electrical outlets: the metallic surface film may conduct electricity, so be sure the power is off in the work area. Consider professional hangers for foil.

- **Flocks** have a fiber facing that resembles velvet, so they are difficult to brush and the seams should not be rolled. Flocks are hard to clean: avoid getting adhesive on the face of flocked wall covering.

- **Embossed** wall coverings have a raised pattern finish that provides a shadow texture to the surface, plus a formal look for use in dining areas or living rooms. You cannot use a seam roller on embossed coverings.

- **Grasscloths** are actually vinyl wall coverings with a surface of hand-tied grass stems. The grass has a flat finish that does not reflect light, plus a rough surface texture, so grasscloth can be used to cover up rough wall surfaces. Be very careful not to get adhesives on the grass, because it is not washable. Use a clear adhesive for hanging grasscloths.

Rather than trying to figure how much wall covering you need, take the room measurements along to the dealer and let him figure the number of rolls needed for your job. Because wall coverings are not uniform in their coverage per roll, it is easy for the d-i-y'er to underestimate the amount of wall covering needed. You can estimate that there will be about 15 percent waste on any wall covering job, because of normal cutting waste. It is important that you buy enough covering to do the job, because the same wall covering will vary in color when taken from another job or dye lot. Also, buy enough wall covering so that you have leftovers for repairs if your wall covering should become damaged in the future.

WALL COVERING TOOLS

Wall covering tools you will need for your job include:

- Water tray for soaking prepasted covering
- Wash pail to hold clean wash water
- Razor knife with snap-off blade tips
- Wall covering scissors
- 6-inch broadknife
- Smoothing brushes
- Plastic smoothing tool
- Seam roller
- Paint tray and paint roller for applying adhesive
- Straightedge (Bubblestick)
- Sponge
- Stepladder
- Towels
- Large tabletop or professional papering table (can be rented)

Tips for Using Tools

The professional paperhanger not only owns the proper tools to do a given job, he knows the secrets of proper tool use. Review the following tips for using tools to avoid some of the frustrations that can arise if good tool techniques are not followed.

- Use the water tray for soaking prepasted coverings. This will activate the adhesive on the back of the coverings. In most cases, the adhesive on the covering will be sufficient to ensure a good bond between the wall covering and the wall or ceiling. But for very difficult surfaces, such as a rough or sand-float surface (which looks like you glued sand particles to the surface and then painted over it), you may want to use additional adhesive. Most manufacturers scoff at this, protesting that the adhesive is adequate as supplied. But some professionals find they need to use more adhesive in special cases. The way to do this is to cut the covering to length and lay the strips out on the table. Then add one quart of the proper adhesive to one gallon of water. Instead of dipping the covering in the water tray, roll the back side of the covering with a paint roller, which has dipped in the water/adhesive mix. Then fold or book the covering and let it set a few minutes, or for the soak time indicated on the wall covering you are installing. This technique will let you take the wall covering to the wall with an extra margin of adhesive.

- Use a razor knife with multiple or breakaway blade tips, and snap off the tip frequently to be sure the cutting tip is always sharp. Cutting against plaster or trim can dull the blade tip with one single cut. A dull blade can snag and tear or even ruin the wall covering strip. Don't skimp on razor blades — dull blades can ruin your wall covering job.

- Turn off the electricity in the room you are papering. If you need lights or power tools in the area, use an extension cord from another circuit to supply power to the work room. The covering with which you will be working will be wet; your hands and tools will be wet; you may be handling metallic (foil) coverings that will conduct electricity. For all these reasons, don't work around live electrical wires when installing wall covering.

- Keep a bath towel handy and dry your hands frequently. Sharp tools such as the razor knife can slip when your hands are wet and cause damage to the wall covering or injury to the worker.

- Use a 6-inch wide broad knife, or a wider 12-inch knife, to fold the covering into the corner(s) and serve as a cutting guide. The blade/guide will help you make a clean, straight cut.

- Begin at the center of the wall covering strip and, working outward to both sides of the strip, use the plastic smoothing tool and the smoothing brushes to remove the wrinkles from the wall covering. If you can't work the wrinkles out, pull the covering away from the wall, straighten it, press it against the wall and try again to smooth it. Don't worry about the covering drying before you can get it smoothed: most adhesives have thirty minutes or more of "open time" to apply and smooth the covering before it dries.

- Excess water and adhesive can be removed from the wall covering using a natural sponge or a quality plastic sponge. Rinse the sponge frequently to clean off any adhesive that has been picked up from the covering.

- Fill the wash pail with clean, warm water, rinse the wash sponge frequently, and dump and refill the wash pail to ensure that the wash water is clean and free from adhesives.

- Choose a stepladder that is adequate to support your weight. Lightweight household stepladders may not support a person who weighs more than 200 pounds, and a broken ladder can result in serious injury.

Adhesives

Your wall covering dealer can guide you to the proper wall covering adhesive for hanging your

Cut a piece of wall covering so that the pattern on the repair piece matches the pattern at the location of the damage. Carefully align the patch so the pattern matches. Photo by the author.

Use masking tape to tape the patch in place. Use a sharp razor knife to cut through both the patch and the existing damaged wall covering. Make cuts on pattern lines so cuts will not be visible. Photo by the author.

particular product. For most vinyl and vinyl-backed wall coverings you can use heavy-duty wall covering adhesive. If you will be installing borders or any vinyl over other vinyl covering, such as where the vinyl wall covering will overlap at inside corners, use a vinyl-over-vinyl adhesive. For hanging grasscloth, flocks, or fabrics, use clear vinyl adhesive. Clear vinyl adhesives will not stain fabric or grasscloth surfaces. Consult your dealer if you have any questions about which adhesive to use.

Preparation

Walls or ceilings to be covered should be free of cracks, loose plaster, and other defects that might reflect through the new wall covering. Although wall covering can cover minor surface defects, the best job will result if the surface is as smooth as possible. Inspect the surface(s) carefully and do all necessary repairs before proceeding (see Chapter 4, Patching Walls and Ceilings).

When the surfaces to be covered are patched and sound, apply a latex primer such as Metylan Prime Coat. If you are preparing new wallboard for wall covering, apply a coat of latex paint or First Coat primer (made by United States Gypsum) followed by a coat of wall sizing, then proceed with wall covering application.

INSTALLING WALL COVERINGS

Before beginning to hang wall coverings review our Tips for Using Tools, above. To ensure a professional-looking job, it is important to follow those tips throughout the installation process. Remember that if you have never installed wall covering, it is best to begin your hanging experience by (1) beginning in a room that has simple lines and angles, with no complicated obstacles to fit around; (2) using prepasted, pretrimmed wall covering; and (3) choosing a wall covering pattern that will not be difficult to match.

Using a carpenter's level, check the corners of the room for plumb. Most corners, especially in older

plastered houses, will be slightly irregular or out of plumb (level on the vertical plane). We will tell you how to compensate for any slight corner irregularities, but corners that are badly out of plumb make matching wall covering patterns difficult at the corners. If corners are badly out of plumb you may choose to hire a professional to hang the wall coverings.

Choose a time to apply the wall covering when you can control the temperature and humidity of the room. The temperature should be no higher than 70 degrees, both for worker comfort and to retard the drying of the wall covering adhesive. If necessary, set a humidifier in the work area to raise humidity levels and retard adhesive drying.

View the room to be covered from the entry door. In most cases you will start hanging at the corner farthest from the entry. Often the room dimensions dictate that there will be a mismatch in the pattern at the final or closing seam: plan the layout so that this final seam will occur over a door or window header, where it will not be noticeable.

Measure the width of the wall covering and subtract $1/2$ inch from the width. Now measure from the corner this distance — covering width minus $1/2$ inch — and make a pencil mark on the wall at that point. Make three measurements: at the top, middle, and bottom of the corner, and make pencil marks at all three points. Use a carpenter's level or a Bubblestick to check to see if the three marks are aligned on the plumb line. If the three marks are not aligned, meaning the corner is crooked, choose the pencil mark that is nearest to the corner — as revealed by the plumb line — and use the Bubblestick and pencil to mark a plumb line from the ceiling to the baseboard.

Before cutting the wall covering, reroll it so the pattern side is in, checking the pattern and color as you reroll. Now cut the wall covering strip, being sure to allow for the drop or pattern repeat. (The drop will be marked on the wall covering package.) In most cases the wall covering will overlap the wall by at least 2 inches both at the ceiling and at the baseboard. Make sure there is a full pattern at the top of the strip.

Now roll the strip with the pattern side in and set it in the plastic water tray. Note the soak time recommended on your wall covering (usually about one minute) and follow it closely to be sure the adhesive on the back of the strip is activated. Remove the strip from the water tray and book it — fold the top of the strip down and the bottom of the strip up so the strip ends meet at the center — so the wall covering will prevent air from reaching the adhesive while it is curing. When the adhesive is fully activated or cured, apply the covering to the wall.

Carry the strip to the wall in the folded or booked position. Unfold the top portion of the strip and position it so there is a full pattern at the top of the wall, the outside edge of the strip matches the plumb line you have marked, and there is a strip overlap of ¹/₂ inch or more at the corner. Use the smoothing brush, working from the center of the strip outward, to smooth the top of the strip. Then unfold the bottom of the strip and push it in position against the plumb line with the palms of your hands. Now use the brush or plastic smoothing tool to smooth the entire strip. Be careful not to stretch the wall covering while you are smoothing it: stretched vinyl will contract as it dries on the wall, and the wall covering seams will open up. Using the broad knife as a guide, trim the overlapping wall covering at both the ceiling and the baseboard. Use the sponge and warm clean water to clean any adhesive off the face of the wall covering and the baseboard or trim.

Now cut the next strip and wet and book it as you did the first. Let it cure, then apply the strip to the wall. Unfold the top of the covering and position it at the ceiling, matching the pattern of the new strip to the pattern of the adjoining strip. Smooth and trim as before.

Continue across the wall until you reach the corner. When you are within less than one strip's width from the corner, measure the distance between the edge of the last strip hung and the corner, and add ¹/₂ inch. This extra ¹/₂ inch will fold around the corner, and will allow for any variation in the plumb of the corner. Prepare the strip and let it cure, then align the edges of the booked strip. Mark the measurement of the width from the last strip to the wall plus the ¹/₂-inch. Use the Bubblestick or carpenter's level as a straightedge to cut the strip for width, and save the cutoff portion of the strip. Install the corner strip, fold the edge around the corner, and smooth the strip as before.

Measure the width of the cutoff strip remnant and then measure that distance from the corner down the wall. Use the Bubblestick to establish a plumb line at that point. Now hang the cutoff strip, matching the pattern at the corner and overlapping the ceiling and baseboard. Smooth and trim the strip as before. This procedure — overlapping each strip at the corner, and establishing a plumb line for the edge of the first strip on each wall — guarantees no wall covering gaps at the corners and ensures that all wall covering strips are plumb, regardless of how plumb the walls or corners are.

If you have a plumb outside corner, you can simply wrap the wall covering strip around the corner and trim. If the outside corner is not plumb, you can wrap the outside corner the same way you do an inside corner, but allow about 1 inch, not ¹/₂ inch, on outside corners.

Do not try to cut strips for windows freehand. Instead, prepare the strip(s) as before, and hang the full strip so it overlaps the window or door. Use the smoothing brush to smooth the wall covering up to the edge of opening trim. Then use the scissors to make a diagonal or 45-degree miter cut on the wall covering, at each corner of the opening trim. Turn back the excess wall covering and use the broad knife to fold it tightly against the edge of the trim. Use the razor knife to trim away the excess covering.

As you proceed with the job, go back after 30 minutes and inspect the wall covering you have hung. Check the seams to be sure they have not

Remove the patch overlay and soak the cutaway damaged area to soften the wall covering adhesive. Carefully peel the damaged portion away from the wall. Photo by the author.

Wet the back of the patch (if prepasted) or apply wall covering adhesive to the back of the patch. Carefully fit the patch material in the area where you removed the damaged covering. Use a clean wet sponge to smooth the patch and to remove any adhesive from the patch. Photo by the author.

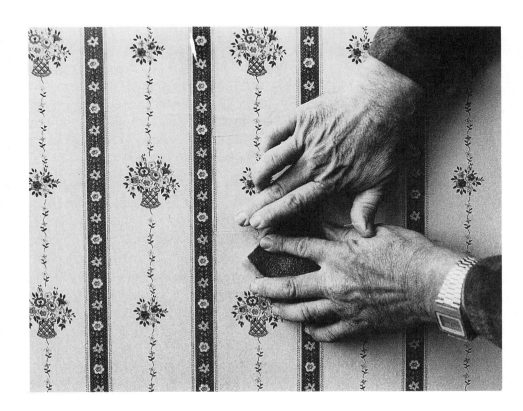

opened. If the wall covering has shrunk and the seams have opened, you may be able to move the covering slightly and close up any gaps at the seams. Roll the seams gently with the seam roller to ensure that the edges of the seams are in contact with the adhesive and will not curl as they dry. Looking down an oblique angle against a sidelight, check the surface of the wall covering for any obvious bubbles or for adhesive on the surface of the wall covering. Use the sponge to wipe off still-soft adhesive, and use the razor knife to make a small slit over any bubbles in the covering. Then inject some adhesive under the bubble, using a glue injector you can buy from your wall covering dealer or a small brush, to put more adhesive under the bubble. Smooth the bubble area and wipe away any excess adhesive with the sponge.

To cut an opening over an electrical outlet, use the razor knife to carefully cut an "X" in the wall covering, over the outlet. Fold the points of the "X" back and cut along each edge of the outlet with the razor knife.

Hanging Borders

Wall covering borders can make attractive accents when used either with paint or with wall covering. Buy borders in complementary or contrasting colors or patterns and install them around the ceiling/wall corner, at chair rail height (32 inches up from the floor) or to form a frame around a window, door, or archway opening. You can cut your own borders by shopping wall covering sales and picking up bargain rolls of regular wall covering. Then cut your own borders from the wall covering.

To hang borders, first decide their location and use a level or a Bubblestick to establish a level line around the room. Mark the level line with a pencil to avoid picking up ink from a ballpoint pen or chalk from a chalkline.

Begin hanging the border at a corner, and overlap the end of the border 1/2 inch onto the adjoining wall. Wet the adhesive and let the border cure, then hang,

using ordinary wall covering application procedures. For making an inconspicuous joint on long walls, overlap two pieces of border so the patterns match, then cut through both layers of border with a sharp razor knife. Use a smoothing brush and a seam roller to smooth and conceal the seam.

REMOVING WALL COVERING

One fairly recent development in wall covering will be welcomed by professional and homeowner alike. For several years now, most of the wall coverings installed have been strippable or peelable. Removing wall covering can be a hot, dirty, sweaty job. It can not only be hard physical work but, if you use a wall covering steamer, it is also work done in a humid and disagreeable environment. So, within a decade or so, we should have seen the last of the old scrape-and-steam wall covering of yesteryear.

Strippable coverings use a release-type adhesive that lets you pull the covering away from the wall, leaving little behind to clean up except adhesive residue. Peelable coverings have a release between the vinyl covering and a paper backing, so you can pull away the vinyl and remove the paper backing by soaking it with hot water or a covering removal product such as Savogran's Fast Wallpaper Remover. Be sure you buy either strippable or peelable wall covering to eliminate the onerous task of steaming off wall covering should you decide to redecorate in the future.

To remove existing wall covering, you should first test it to see if it is strippable or peelable. Just use a broad knife or paint scraper to lift a corner of the wall covering. Pull up in a steady pull, and strippable/peelable wall covering should easily come away from the wall. Then you have only to remove the residue on the wall before you redecorate. If the wall covering was strippable and left only adhesive residue, add a little Savogran's Fast Wallpaper Remover to warm water and use a plastic pot scrubber or sponge to clean the old adhesive residue from the wall. If the wall covering is peelable and leaves a thin layer of paper backing on the wall, plus the adhesive residue, you must work a bit harder with the warm water/Fast solution. Apply the remover solution with a sponge, let it sit until the adhesive is softened, and then use a broad knife or scraper to remove the paper and adhesive residue. Be sure to let the remover solution work and do its job before you begin to scrape the wall: the scraping is the hard part if you attack the job before the solution has had time to soften the old adhesive. The task should not be that difficult if you give the remover time to work.

One good rule is to cover the floor with layers of newspapers to catch and soak up the mess. Plastic is slippery: if you put down plastic, put it down *first*, under the newspapers. Tape the edges of the plastic to the baseboard so water cannot run down the wall and under the plastic or newspaper covering.

If you already have the old-style wallpaper, you will have to do the old paper remover act. This means wetting the adhesive until it softens, either via steam from a steamer or hot water/remover solution via a sponge or sponge mop, and then using a broad knife to scrape the goop off the wall. If the covering is truly paper, even many layers of old paper, you can readily soak through to the adhesive using a wallpaper remover solution. If the wall covering is vinyl, you will have to abrade or scratch through the paper using a tool such as the Paper Tiger, a tool with a serrated wheel that will punch a series of small holes in the surface so the moisture from the remover solution can penetrate through the surface and reach the adhesive.

If you bring up the subject of wallpaper removal in the presence of most homeowners, you will elicit a chorus of moans and groans. As bad as it all sounds, removing wallpaper or other wall covering is not that tough a job, if you do it right. I once removed all the wall covering from a five-room house in a half-day (four hours) using nothing but a pail, a sponge mop, and a scraper.

Removing paper or wall covering correctly to us

means not using a steamer and not attacking the wallpaper or covering until the adhesive is completely softened. By *softened* we do not mean you can chip it off the wall: the adhesive is softened when you can position the broad knife or scraper at the baseboard and, in one continuous movement, can push the scraper up the wall and remove the wall covering to bare plaster. If you are just chipping away and removing small patches of paper, you have not softened the adhesive yet and should apply more water and wait.

The key is patience. The process is as follows. Mix warm water with Savogran's Fast or other wallpaper remover, according to label directions. Use a sponge or sponge mop to apply the remover solution. Wear rubber gloves and eye goggles to protect your hands and eyes from the remover solution.

Turn off the furnace thermostat and close up the room to prevent drafts and evaporation of the remover solution. If the humidity level in the house is low, place a humidifier in the room and close the doors and windows. Turn the humidifier high and get the air good and damp in the room. This will help hold the remover on the wall, so it can soak into the paper.

Now use the sponge to wet down an entire wall. Not a small spot, the *entire wall*. It takes a long time for the remover solution to soak through the paper to the adhesive, then to soften the adhesive. This is not a five-minute interval. Give it time. Apply the remover solution to the wall and you will see the wallpaper will soak up this first solution application like a blotter. When you have soaked one wall, go back and apply another treatment of solution. In this manner apply the solution to all four walls in a small bedroom, at least two walls of a larger room. When the remover solution is absorbed into the wallpaper, it will look wet enough to remove. It is not. All you are seeing is a surface wetting of the paper: the adhesive is still hard. Keep soaking until the adhesive is turned to thin jelly. After you have soaked a wall several times, with a few minutes wait between each application of remover solution, try to scrape the paper away. If the paper comes off easily, in large sheets, you have wet the wall enough and you can remove the paper. If you have to chip away small bits of the paper, you just don't have the wallpaper wet enough. Wet it again, take a break, then wet it again. Would you rather soak it off or scrape it off? Patience!

It helps to have a helper for this repetitive task: wet, soak, rewet, soak, scrape takes a lot of elbow grease. But even working alone, you can remove a lot of paper if you take your time and let the remover do the work.

Another time saver is to keep a plastic garbage pail or trash bag handy, and put the old wall covering in the trash container as you remove it. The old covering will quickly pile up on the floor and become a slippery, gooey mess to walk on or over. Keep cleanup to a minimum by keeping debris picked up as you go: don't drop it on the floor and come back later to clean up.

12
Floors

The floor system of your house is supported by the floor joists and bridging, perhaps with a central beam or support wall to hold everything up in the center. The floor system consists of a layer of 3/4-inch or 1 x 6 board subfloor (if the house was built anytime up to the mid-1950s) or 1/2-inch plywood subfloor (if your house was built anytime after the mid-1950s, when use of plywood sheathing became common). Over this subfloor is a layer of builder's paper, sometimes called red rosin paper, and then a finish floor. The finish floor may be hardwood, or it may be another layer of plywood (called underlayment) with a floor covering of some kind laid atop the underlayment.

The purpose of this head-bone-connected-to-the-neck-bone litany is to point out that a floor system is made up of many components — floor joists, support walls or beams, bridging, subfloor, and finish floor — and movement occurs between each and all of these components. As that movement occurs, weird noises such as squeaks, squeals, shrieks, and groans may go bump in the night, disturbing your peace.

The floors also take a beating. They support a lot of weight, including the weight of the occupants, furniture, and appliances. This is called the "live load." If you will check the floor joists of your house from the underside (from crawlspace or basement), you will see that the builder often used double joists to support extraordinary loads. You may see doubled floor joists at the point in the kitchen floor directly below the refrigerator and range. The doubled joists support the extra weight of the appliances. You may

also see doubled joists alongside openings, such as stairwells cut into the floor, or under partitions, bathtubs, or anyplace the floor may be called upon to carry any extra load.

You will also likely see *bridging* positioned at the midpoint between each pair of floor joists. The bridging may be solid wood, a pair of 1 x 2 wood boards set in an "X" between the joists, or metal "X" bracing between the floor joists. The bridging is so-called because it is like the "X" bracing used under bridge decks. Bridging is intended to stiffen the floor by transferring the loading from joist to joist. Bridging also helps prevent the floor joists from twisting and warping as they dry out or "settle" after construction. In recent years, building officials have decided that bridging is not needed at midspan on rooms that are 12 feet wide or less. Some home writers concluded from this decision that bridging in fact was not doing its job, i.e., stiffening the floor. All that was really decided was that, because of modern methods of rating the load capacity of floor joists, builders need not spend the time and money to place bridging between floor joists that are less than 12 feet long. Bridging still will transfer floor loads and prevent the spring or bounce that is common on older floors.

If your house is older, pre-World War II, you may have floor joists that are not strong enough to support the floor load. In those days, particularly in rural areas, lumber was often home-cut in the woodlot, and a 2 x 12 was considered to be a 2 x 12. Farmer Brown did not use a sophisticated lumber-grading system, and that is why sagging floors were

Trus-Joist manufactured floor joists permit the lumber industry to make more efficient use of wood products than solid lumber joists do. The joists combine a web of oriented strand board with flanges of laminated veneer lumber to offer a strong, squeak-free floor. The joists also offer ease of handling: note the two workmen positioning a lightweight 26-foot long joist that spans the entire width of the house. Courtesy of Trus-Joist Corp.

a common problem in older houses. From modern testing, we now know that there is a wide discrepancy between the strength and load limits of various species and grades of wood. Joists are rated to reflect the floor load they will support over a given span. (The span is the distance between two support walls or beams.) For example, size for joist size, spruce lumber is stronger than white pine. A 2 x 12 floor joist of No. 2 Eastern White Pine, spaced 16 inches on center (o.c.) will support a floor load over a span of only 17-4 feet, but a 2 x 12 of Select Structural Eastern Spruce can support a floor load over a wider 21-6 foot span. Thus, joist span tables must consider not only the dimension of the lumber (2 x 12) but also consider the species and grade of the joist. If you would install the No. 2 Eastern White Pine 2 x 12 to hold a span of 21-6 feet, a span that could be handled by an Eastern Spruce 2 x 12, you would likely have a sagging floor.

Today, manufactured joists such as the web-joist system used by Trus Joist Corporation go Mother Nature one better. Trus Joists use intermediate webs of oriented strand board (OSB) and grooved edge flanges of laminated veneer lumber to take the bounce and the squeaks out of modern floors. If you are remodeling or building anew, by all means specify Trus Joist manufactured floor joists for your floor system.

SQUEAKING FLOORS

Who has squeaking floors? If one judges by the number of query letters sent to how-to magazine editors, everyone has them, because squeaking floors are a most common complaint. One chief editor, new to the job, observed that, had he not counted the volume personally, he would not have believed the homeowner interest in curing squeaking floors. Perhaps the wide interest is due to the fact that it can be hard to find and cure a squeak in the floor.

To find squeaks in the floor, have one person walk on the floor above while another waits in the basement or crawlspace and listens for squeaks. The listener then can use chalk to make an "X" to mark the squeak area so you can come back later and remedy the squeak.

First, when you walk across the floor and cause it to flex or vibrate, any wood flooring member can rub against another and cause a squeak. In older houses, where you have tongue-and-groove hardwood flooring laid atop a wood subfloor, the floor layer may have omitted using the red rosin builder's paper between the floor and subfloor, so you have hardwood flooring rubbing against wood subfloors and causing a squeak. The cure can be to drive wallboard screws upwards through the subfloor and into the hardwood flooring in the squeak area, from the basement or crawlspace side. This will pull the two layers of wood together so they will not flex when you walk across the floor. Be careful to use screws that are not long enough to penetrate all the way through both layers of flooring. You don't want the screw to pop up on the finished surface of the floor. Use screws that are no more than 1 1/4 inch long. If the basement ceiling is finished, so you cannot reach the underside of the subfloor, there is no way you can drive the screws so they will be concealed. You can have a professional come in and test the floor for squeaks, then drive flooring nails at an angle through the hardwood flooring and sink the heads. You can then putty the nail holes and conceal them. If you have carpet over hardwood floors, carpet replacement time, while the hardwood floor is exposed, is the right time to nail down any floor squeaks. One thing to keep in mind about squeaks: try to isolate the squeak area before you begin repairs. Many times people just begin to drive nails or screws randomly over a wide area of the floor, and end up with a floor peppered with unsightly fasteners. Drive a fastener or two and walk over the squeak area: often, just that fastener or two will cure the squeak.

Check the floor bridging. If wood bridging is placed against adjoining members in the "X" or cross bridging, one piece of bridging may be rubbing against another as the floor flexes when you walk across it. In this case you can just tap one member of the bridging with a hammer and drive it slightly away from the other bridging, so there is a slight gap between them and rubbing is eliminated.

If you eliminate the bridging and interfloor friction as the squeak source, check to see whether there may be a gap between the subfloor and the floor joists. Use a small prybar to test for tightness between the subfloor and the joists. If you can easily pry up the subfloor, you can insert wood shims between the subfloor and the joists to cure the loose flooring and prevent the squeaks.

One word of caution: Many tool rental stores will rent floor sanders, and most do-it-yourself texts proclaim that sanding floors is within the talents of the d-i-y'er. I disagree: I have written texts telling people the basics of running a sander (because some will try it, no matter what), but as a former contractor I do not consider sanding floors to be work for amateurs. It takes a practiced touch, in my opinion, to sand a floor successfully. Aside from the problems of getting a smooth floor when you don't know how to operate a floor sander, there is another problem. If you remove too much stock (wood) from the floor you may start it squeaking where it did not squeak before sanding. And if that is the unhappy result, there is nothing you can do, short of laying a new floor, to get rid of the squeaks.

Be aware that some noises you hear may not be floor squeaks but may be caused by components other than the flooring. For example, sheet metal ducts may be nailed tightly to the floor joist(s) and you may hear a "tin-can" noise — the kind of noise you hear when you flex the bottom of a tin can. In some cases you can loosen the nails or the support brackets from the floor joists and stop the noise. The same is true of plumbing pipes that are slung underneath floor joists using pipe hangers, V-shaped wire hangers that support pipes. If the pipe hangers are set too tight, so the pipes are clamped tightly against the joist bottoms, the pipes may squeak against the

wood joists when the floor flexes, the hot water pipes expand or contract, or the pipes vibrate from water flow. Again, loosen the pipe clamps so the pipes can move freely against the joists and you may cure the noise. Or insert insulation or plastic pads between the pipes and the joists to cushion the movement and reduce the noise. You can also push fiberglass insulation into pipe holes in the joists or studs to stop hammering or other pipe noises.

SAGGING FLOORS

Sagging floor joists are most often due to use of undersized floor joists in the original construction. Because of modern lumber grading and national mortgage experience, in which agencies such as FHA and VA have observed housing problems over the decades, strict building standards and codes have been established, and as a result one sees fewer sagged floors and ceilings in modern houses. The use of roof trusses and floor web trusses has also resulted in stiffer joists and less sag or deflection in both ceiling and floor joists.

If you can drop a marble on the floor and watch it roll to the center of the room, your floors have a decided sag and should be jacked up and leveled. This is not terribly difficult to do, for anyone who has some carpentry experience, but you alone should be the judge of whether your physical condition and building experience are such that you can successfully do this repair yourself, or whether you should have professionals do the work. Tools you will need include a heavy hydraulic jack and a 4 x 4 post cut to reach between the bottom edge of the floor joists and the top of the hydraulic jack, as it sits on the basement floor or the ground beneath the crawlspace. Understand that you must position the 4 x 4 post with care: any post that slips sideways or "kicks back" as the pressure increases from the jack being raised can fly out with great force and with possible injury to the worker(s).

Check the floor from the bottom side to judge the degree of sag in the floor joists. You can use a straightedge such as a straight 2 x 4, 8 feet long, to check each joist for sag. The joists will deflect or sag along the length, with maximum amount of sag occurring at the exact center of the joist, and the greatest sag (usually, depending on the live loading on the floor) at the center joist of the floor. Just position the 2 x 4 straightedge directly under the middle of any joist, holding the center of the 2 x 4 tight against the bottom edge of the joist. Check to see how much sag you have by checking how much gap there is between the joist and straightedge at each end of the 2 x 4. If you split the difference between the ends, so that the gap is equal at each end of the 2 x 4 straight edge, you can judge how much you will have to jack up the middle of the sagged joist to make it straight again. If you have a sag of one inch or so at the center of the joist, it will not require much jacking to bring the joist straight. If the maximum sag or deflection appears to be more than one inch at the center of the room, you may want to call in a contractor to straighten the sagged floors.

To support the floors after straightening and leveling them, you will have to install new joists, the same size as the existing joists, alongside the sagged joists. Count the sagged joists and measure them for length, and buy an equal number of matching joists. For example, if you have 2 x 8 joists, 12 feet long, buy new joists to match. Be sure to buy the joists exactly as long as the sagged joists, i.e., long enough to overlap and rest upon the basement or foundation wall at one end and upon the center support wall or beam. Also buy a few pounds of 16d nails to nail the new joists to the old sagged joists. The number of nails needed will depend on the size of your floor and the number of joists. You will also need a saw and a carpenter's hammer.

Note that the existing joists will have shrunk during the settling process and may be up to $1/2$ inch narrower than the new joists. Then you will have to use a plane or a saw to notch the ends of the new joists, where they sit over the support walls.

If necessary, cut a new joist to length to match the existing joist. Notch the ends if you must to make them fit atop the support walls. Remove any bridging between the joists. You are now ready to begin jacking up the joists.

You can rent heavy-duty jacks. Set the hydraulic jack under a sagged joist nearest the outside edge of the room. Position the 4 x 4 post squarely under the center of the sagged joist and atop the hydraulic jack. Use a carpenter's level to be sure the post and jack are aligned squarely under the joist, and the 4 x 4 post is plumb, to avoid a kick-back and injury from the 4 x 4 post.

Slowly begin the jacking process. Keep an eye on the 4 x 4 post and stop jacking if the 4 x 4 post appears to slip. Release the tension on the jack and realign the 4 x 4 post before beginning to jack the joist again. Raise the sagged joist about $1/4$ inch, then wait a few minutes. If the joists are very old, they will be brittle and prone to cracking. Listen for any cracking sound in the joist. You may need to stop jacking and let the sagged joist "rest" overnight before continuing to jack it upwards, to avoid splitting dry, brittle joists.

If there is no sign of splitting in the joist, and no sounds to indicate damage to plaster or wallboard above, continue jacking up the joist. Check when you think you have jacked the joist straight again: use the 2 x 4 straightedge set along the bottom side of the joist to check for level. Keep jacking until the bottom is straight or slightly above being level at the center.

Now install the new joist alongside the existing joist, and be sure that the ends of the new joist overlap and rest on the supports at both joist ends. The new joist should be a tight fit and may need to be levered into place against the old joist. When the new joist is tight against the old joist, spike the two joists together. Drive the 16d nails through the new joist and into the old joist, positioning them in threes at the top, center, and bottom of the joists across the width and about 16 inches apart (o.c.) along the length of the joists.

When you have spiked the new joist into place, lower the jack and move it and the 4 x 4 post to the next joist. Repeat the procedure, jacking the joist at the center and raising it up to level. When the sagged joist is raised to level or slightly high (just 1/8 to 1/4 inch crowned: the joist may come down that much when you lower the jack) cut and position a new joist alongside the sagged joist. Spike the two joists together as before, being sure that each end of the new joist is supported at the ends by the support walls/beam.

In the same manner, continue across the room, jacking and doubling up the floor joists as you go. When you have doubled up the joists at all locations, the floor will be level and stiff, and it will not sag again.

SQUEAKING STAIRS

The staircase, usually referred to simply as the stairs, is made up of a number of components. The long boards that stretch between two floors and support the steps are called the *stringers*; the flat part of the step is called the *tread*; the face material below the tread is called the *riser*. Note that some stairs have open treads, with no riser to cover the face of the stringer. As with the floor structure itself, there are many components to a staircase, and if any of the components moves and rubs against another component the staircase may develop annoying squeaks.

As with the floors, the best plan is to position one person under the stairs while a second person climbs the stairs. The person doing the stair climbing should test each tread with his/her weight, stepping at the center of the tread. If this does not produce a squeak, the climber can then step on either side of the tread, where the tread butts against the stringers. When a squeak is heard you can mark its location.

If the squeak is heard on only one or two treads you have narrowed the possible sources. The tread is flexing under the climber's weight and is rubbing against the riser above the tread, which rests atop

the tread; the riser below the tread upon which the front edge of the tread rests; or one of the three stringers.

If the bottom side of the staircase is unfinished and accessible, you can cut small blocks of wood and apply carpenter's wood glue to the wood blocks on two sides. Then position a wood block in each corner formed by the front riser and the tread above. You may need to secure these wood blocks in place with small nails until the glue dries and locks the two pieces together so they cannot move and squeak. Avoid using the stairs until the glue sets, usually within hours (see the label directions).

Another option to quiet stairs is to drill holes through the underside of the tread, up into the edge of the riser above. Drive screw shank (threaded) flooring nails into the predrilled holes to tie the risers to the treads.

If the stair treads are not carpeted, you can predrill holes in the tops of the treads and drive screw shank flooring nails through the top of the treads and into the stringers or into the edges of the risers beneath. If the stair treads are carpeted, you can live with the squeak until time to recarpet, then take care of any squeaks when you remove the old carpet. Or, if the squeak is very annoying, have the carpet layer remove the carpet from the steps, take care of the squeaks, then reinstall the carpet.

HARDWOOD FLOORS

To any old-timer, hardwood floors mean oak or maple tongue-and-groove strips laid over red rosin paper and subflooring, then filled, sanded, and finished on the job. The modern, factory-finished strip flooring commonly used today we refer to as prefinished flooring.

Hardwood flooring is cut from kiln-dried wood at the factory, and if it is properly handled and installed it is reasonably stable. Still, most wood products have some degree of expansion/contraction, and the installer must make allowances for this movement. This means that narrow gaps are left at all sides of the room, to allow the flooring to expand

Floor noises can often be traced to plumbing pipes that rub against pipe hangers or to floor bridging that rubs when people walk across the floor. Adjust pipe hangers and floor bridging to stop these noises. Photo by the author.

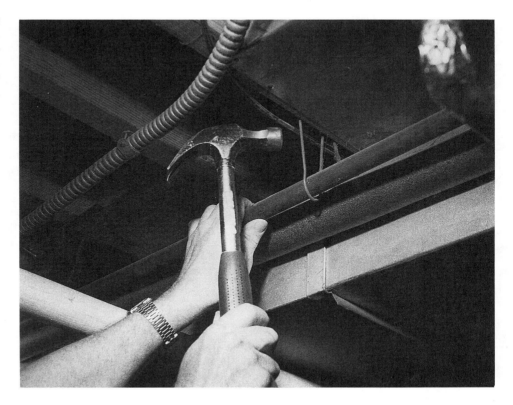

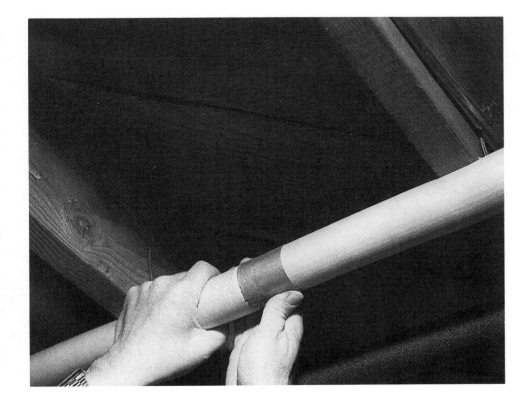

Noisy plumbing pipes can often be silenced by wrapping the pipes with foam pipe insulation. Photo by the author.

under the base molding. If the flooring is laid tightly wall-to-wall, it will expand and buckle during periods of high humidity. The point is that you should know what you are doing to lay unfinished hardwood flooring.

If you have squeaks in hardwood flooring, and you are sure the squeaks are not in the subfloor or floor joists but in the flooring itself, you can drive wallboard screws upwards through the subfloor to secure the flooring in place. Some of that flooring was laid by people who were paid "piecework" or worked by the square foot. Some, in order to lay more flooring per day, skimped on the nailing and nailed every second board, letting the tongue-and-grooves hold the unnailed flooring boards in place. These floors, improperly nailed, almost surely will squeak. We have discussed how to "blind nail" or screw the flooring from the underside so as not to mar the beauty of the hardwood surface. But if the poor workmanship is widespread, with much of the flooring unnailed or with no rosin paper between the hardwood and the subfloor to keep them from rubbing and squeaking together, the only alternative may be to have a professional take up the flooring and re-lay it properly.

Hardwood flooring is not really difficult to maintain, although much of it was covered by carpeting in the '50s and '60s. The generations that grew up on the carpeted floors of the past decades have rediscovered the beauty of hardwood. If you have prefinished wood floors, follow the manufacturers' maintenance directions provided with the flooring. Most hardwood requires only that you keep it free of dirt and grit that could scratch the finish. Sweep the floor or use an electric broom to pick up dirt and grit from the flooring. The most durable hardwood flooring finish is polyurethane. Damp-mop polyurethane but do not apply floor wax to it. Floor finishers say that the wax is difficult to remove and may interfere with future finish coats. Have the hardwood floor refinished by a professional if the finish becomes worn or badly damaged.

Minor scratches or gouges in hardwood floors can be filled with latex wood patcher. The wood patcher can be sanded smooth and stained with stain from a patch kit to match the existing floor. For renewing and repairing hardwood floors, I have found the Gillespie Company's line of floor care and repair products, sold at many paint and decorating centers, to be easy to use and to offer superior results.

13
Floor Covering

The construction of floors in wood-floor houses has varied little through the years. The only variation in wood floor construction was a change in 1950 in building materials, when plywood began to replace 1 x 6 boards for use as subfloor sheathing. The floor system of a wood-frame house consists of basement or foundation piers or posts to support a center beam set down the center of the house. Upon the post/beam support rest the floor joists, which are 2 x 8s, 2 x 10s, or 2 x 12s, depending on the width of the house or the span of the joists. At floor openings for stairways, you have doubled or trimmer joists along the length of the opening, and double header joists across the width of the opening. Between the joists may be bridging, used to transfer the loading from joist to joist and to stiffen the floor. Bridging also is intended to prevent the joists from twisting or warping and thus to hold the joists perpendicular to the beams and support walls beneath the joists. This entire structure encompasses the *framing* of the floor.

The next component added is the sheathing or subfloor. If the house was built before 1950, the subfloor sheathing is 1 x 6 or 1 x 8 boards. Board lumber as sheathing ended with the development of plywood, which is both stronger and faster to work with than board lumber. Atop the plywood was laid either strip hardwood flooring or another layer of plywood, which became the underlayment for floor covering such as carpeting or vinyl sheet goods. In most cases, a layer of builder's paper, sometimes called red rosin paper, was laid between the subfloor and the hardwood flooring or the plywood under-

layment. The rosin paper helped to quiet the floor by preventing any friction noises when the floor sheathing and finish flooring moved and rubbed against one another. If the finish flooring was hardwood strips (usually either oak or maple), then hundreds of joints were created between these hardwood strips. To make the circle complete, base molding or shoe molding is nailed around the perimeter of the floor to conceal the crack between the floor and the walls.

The point of this discussion is that each component in this floor structure is a possible source for developing flooring squeaks. Strip hardwood flooring can flex and rub against adjoining strips when the floor is walked upon. Or the strip flooring or plywood can move against the subfloor board or plywood sheathing. The sheathing in turn can move and rub against the floor joists; the floor joists can creak if they can sag under a person's weight; "X" bridging can rub against adjoining bridging and cause squeaks. Before you install new floor covering go back to Chapter 12, Floors, for advice on how to correct squeaking floors, stairs, and other floor problems.

SHEET FLOOR COVERING

A common concern in the floor covering industry has been the danger of asbestos exposure from removing old floor covering. According to the Environmental Protection Agency (EPA), the danger from asbestos is from breathing the airborne asbestos fibers. For this reason, it is thought that the best approach may be simply to leave any material in place rather than removing it. Recently a story has been making the rounds in the floor covering business of a worker who sanded vinyl floors prior to covering over them with new flooring. The house was then inspected for asbestos and it was found that the sanding had spread the particles throughout the house. The homeowner sued the flooring contractor and won. The obvious lesson is that one should never sand existing floor covering to smooth it. Manufacturers are forbidden to use asbestos in new home products, so if you cover over the old product there should be no future danger from asbestos exposure. We will discuss several ways to install new floor covering without removing the old product.

Preparing for New Floor Covering

If the old floor covering is in bad shape, you can install a new underlayment to cover it up. This is the best approach for many reasons. For example, if you remove the old floor covering, the old black adhesive ("cutback") may bleed through the new vinyl floor covering. The best technique is to install a new layer of 1/4-inch thick lauan mahogany plywood over the old flooring. Just nail the plywood in place following the directions of the flooring manufacturer. Then use a floor filler such as "Dependable" to fill and smooth the joints in the plywood. Dependable is a product you will not find at home centers: check in the Yellow Pages for a dealer who sells materials to professional floor covering installers to find Dependable or a similar floor filler product.

If built-in cabinets or appliances make a 3/8-inch (subflooring and covering) rise in the floor level a problem, you can cover directly over the old flooring. Use a wax remover product to remove any floor wax and trowel two coats of Dependable over the entire floor. If the floor covering is embossed, the pattern may show or "photo" through the new floor covering. Ask the pro dealer to supply you with an embossing compound. Apply two or more trowel coats of embossing compound to smooth the surface. Then install the new floor covering.

Inlaid vs. Vinyl

Inlaid products compare in quality to the old linoleum of yesteryear. The product is heavy and is usually available in 6-foot wide rolls because of its weight. This means that you will have extra seams if you install inlaid product. One plus is that the heavy weight of inlaid product translates into durability. Also, the product has the pattern and color continuous through its entire thickness, so any wear is less noticeable. If you choose inlaid product, be sure the installer uses the proper adhesive for the job.

Inlaid products are at the high end of the cost scale, for both the material and the labor. Expect to pay about $30 per square yard for inlaid material, plus around $8 per yard for labor and floor prep. A good example of this superior product might be Armstrong's Designer Solarian.

Many new vinyl floor covering products now approach inlaids in quality. Vinyl floor products have surface or wear layers of up to 20 to 30 mils thickness. Buy a vinyl product with a wear layer thickness of at least 15 mils. Vinyls with thinner wear layers, often called "builder grades," may look good when new but will not provide long wear. Use lighter weight products only in low-traffic areas.

Vinyl floor coverings offer a wide range of colors, patterns, and designs. Because the vinyls are made in 12-foot widths, they are called "seamless" vinyls, and they can be seamless when laid in rooms less than 12 feet wide. There still may be seams at doors or on wider rooms (called "fill"). Be sure the installer uses a seam sealer to weld the material together at the seams. Seams that are not sealed let air or water enter, damaging the adhesive so the edge of the vinyl will curl back and ruin the appearance of the floor. You can see the seam sealer as a continuous 3/16-inch bead of sealer at the seams. Seam sealer will also help conceal the seams in vinyl coverings.

Vinyl Tiles

Vinyl tiles used to be called "vat tile," for "vinyl asbestos tile." Starting in 1980 asbestos was banned from home products, so today they are called "Vct" for "vinyl composition tile."

The drawbacks to using floor tile include the fact that there will be 4 feet of seam per tile. Water from washing floors can seep into the tile seams and will break down the tile adhesive. This is especially common around sink areas in the kitchen or bathroom.

On the plus side, vinyl floor tiles are easy to install, even for the homeowner. The tiles are durable and provide flexibility of design: two colors, checkerboard black and white tile, and freedom in creating borders are possible options for tile. Another plus for vinyl floor tile is ease of repair: damaged tiles can be removed and new tiles put down in their place. Just save a dozen or so tiles for future repairs.

Floor Covering Maintenance

On vinyl tile or inlaid flooring, use a good quality floor wax to protect the flooring and keep floors looking good. Use a water and vinegar solution to clean dirty floors. Apply a good floor wax per manufacturer's instructions. Most waxes will yellow with age: use a wax stripper to remove old wax and recoat with floor wax of your choice. Floor wax is especially needed on vinyl tile floors, because the wax prevents water from entering the joints and attacking the tile adhesive.

"No-wax" vinyl floor products were designed to retain their sheen while eliminating the chore of applying floor wax. On no-wax flooring just damp mop with a solution of warm water and vinegar. Some homemakers prefer to use a "mop and glow" floor product to enhance the gloss or sheen of the floor finish. Be aware that if you apply such products you are applying a thin coat of floor wax, and you will have to use a wax stripper when the product turns yellow with age.

Never lay a padded area rug atop a vinyl floor. Area rugs are often used by sinks or by a kitchen door. The padding on the rug may contain petroleum products that are incompatible with the vinyl flooring and will leave a stain in the vinyl that cannot be removed. The problem is compounded if direct sunlight falls on the rug.

CARPETING

Because they offer a unifying point that ties together all the color and texture in a room, carpeting and other floor covering may be the most important single factors in your decorating scheme. Carpet offers color, texture, floor insulation, underfoot comfort, and easy maintenance. Because carpets are available in such wide color and style options, making a buying decision may be difficult. To ensure that you make the right decision, choose your carpet supplier carefully and take time to learn the basics of carpet construction and care.

Choosing a Carpet Dealer

Finding a reputable carpet outlet should not be difficult. Most national department stores have well-earned reputations for honesty, meaning you will get what you pay for and may even get a bargain if you shop the sales. Local carpet dealers who have served their neighborhoods for years also have earned a place as honest businesses. Be wary of the bargain carpet outlets that profess to undersell their competition. A deal that sounds too good to be true is probably neither good nor true. Ask the salesperson to show you the carpet specification books for any carpet you are interested in. If the dealer cannot supply specification books for his products he may be selling carpet "seconds" or carpets with manufacturing defects. Some carpet defects may be only in the yarn or pattern, but some defects involve problems with adhesives or other materials that could affect the durability of the carpet. If you buy seconds from a discount dealer, you may soon be vacuuming up your carpet investment.

In recent years we have seen a growth in the number of 800-number carpet ads for companies that sell

SAXONY PLUSH

TEXTURED PLUSH	FRIEZE	CUT-LOOP	LEVEL LOOP	MULTI-LEVEL LOOP	RANDOM SHEAR

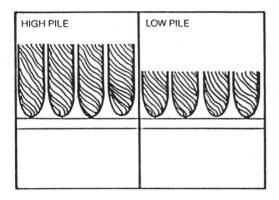

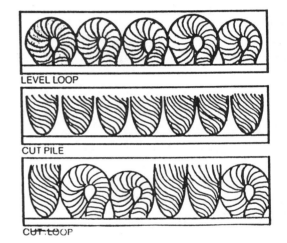

HIGH PILE | LOW PILE

LEVEL LOOP

CUT PILE

CUT-LOOP

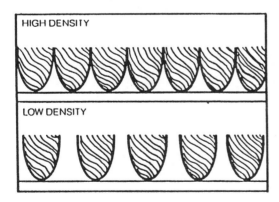

HIGH DENSITY

LOW DENSITY

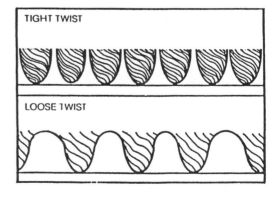

TIGHT TWIST

LOOSE TWIST

The term "carpet styles" refers to the treatment and configuration of the loop or pile of the carpet. Density refers to the stitches per inch or closeness of the fibers; twist refers to the tightness of the wound fibers and contributes to the resistance of a carpet to show tracking or footprints.

carpets by phone. In some cases the carpet dealer will send you carpet samples from which to make your selection. Other dealers ask you to do the legwork in your own community, checking local suppliers' samples so that you can provide the manufacturer with the style and color of the carpet when you call.

Most of these dealers will offer carpets at or near wholesale prices. You will also save the sales tax if you are buying carpet from out of state, but you will have to pay the shipping charges. Many of these carpet-by-phone dealers are in the area around Dalton, Georgia, where the process of tufting was begun and developed to its current state of the art.

When you have decided upon a dealer and have obtained carpet sample books, study the carpet specifications. Note especially the brand name, warranty information, style, density, weight, and pile content of the carpet. These are the factors that can affect carpet quality.

Carpet style — Although woven carpets are still available, most carpets today are made by the tufting process. In this process, tufts of carpet yarn or fiber pierce through the backing material and form the carpet pile. If the pile loops are uniform in size and height, the carpet is called a *level loop pile*. Berber styles, for example, are level loop carpets that have tight loops and maximum fiber density. Carpets with loops of uneven height are called *multi-level loops*. If a carpet has cut loops and even height, the carpet is called a *cut loop*, but if loops are uneven in height and some are cut, the carpet is called a *random shear*. When loops are all cut and are all a uniform 1/2-inch height, the carpet is called a *Saxony*, while the same carpet with a longer pile or loop may be called a *velvet*, *plush*, or *textured plush*.

Carpets that have straight tufts blended with twisted or curled tufts are called *friezes*. These friezes or twists, with their curled tufts, offer a resilient textured pile that resists matting and does not show footprints. These carpets are also called "trackless."

Check to be sure the twisted tufts are heatset to preserve tuft resiliency.

The most durable carpets are the variable loop piles, and they are the best choices for high traffic areas such as halls, stairways, or family rooms.

Density and weight — Density refers to how tightly packed the carpet fibers are, or the number of carpet fibers per square inch. This will be shown in the carpet specification book. Density is shown as "stitches/inch" (spi) or "stitches/3 inches." For residential carpets, expect a density of 9-10 spi; 5 to 6 spi for Berbers; and 10 to 12 spi for level-loop or commercial carpets. After counting the stitches per inch, bend the carpet at a 90 degree angle, as the carpet would be bent around the edge of a stair tread. Look to see how much carpet backing is "peeking" at you. The less visible the backing and the more stitches per inch (higher the pile density) the more durable the carpet will be.

Also, check the carpet's pile yarn weight. For Saxonies, Berbers, or plushes, select a carpet that has not less than 40 ounces pile weight: more pile weight is better. Buy commercial carpet with at least a 26 ounce pile weight. Note that this weight is the weight of the carpet pile only; there will also be listed a total weight of the carpet, which includes not only the weight of the pile but the weight of the carpet backing.

Pile content — Also listed in the specification book will be the type of fiber used in the carpet. The listing may be shown as "pile content," "pile yarn," or simply "pile." This is also an important gauge of carpet durability.

Carpet yarns include nylon, olefin, polyester, polypropylene, and natural fibers such as wool or cotton. Some early polyester pile carpets were prone to matting and early wear, but dealers now say that today's polyesters are durable and more crush-resistant than their early counterparts. Often, polyester fibers are combined in a fiber blend, such as a nylon/polyester carpet.

Olefin may be the most durable of the fibers, but pure olefin is coarse and rough to the touch. To soften the fibers, they are often combined with nylon. Tough Berber carpets are available in nylon/ olefin blends or in pure nylon. Nylon pile combines such features as softness, ease of cleaning, resistance to matting, and good durability, so 100 percent nylon fibers are always a good choice.

Carpet pad — Because the pad cushions the carpet from premature wear and provides underfoot comfort, pad choice is as important as carpet choice. A carpet pad that is too thick may interfere with good balance and may be hazardous to the elderly or infirm. A pad that is too thin will cause premature wear of the carpet and may even cause the carpet seams to split apart. The best way to check a carpet pad is to lay samples of both pad and carpet on the floor, as they would be when laid, and walk or stand on them to test underfoot comfort.

Pad materials include felt, "prime" or single color plastic foam, "rebond" or multi-color foam plastic, and solid rubber pads. For both economy and performance, choose a 6- to 8-pound rebond pad for most of your carpet installations. (Special situations, such as carpeting steps, may call for a thinner, denser pad. Trust your installer's advice.) Rebond pads are made from multi-colored foam particles, bonded together with adhesives. Rebond pads will not "bottom out" or lose their resiliency as inferior pads may do.

Selecting the carpet — When you have read the specifications for the carpet samples, it is time to make your final selection. The first priority is to consider your own lifestyle. A busy family will require carpets that are durable and easy to clean, while a working couple or retirees may prefer a more luxurious carpet with durability a secondary consideration. While halls and stairs require a durable carpet, bathroom carpets must also resist stains and be easy to clean. Ask your dealer if you need help to make the final carpet selection.

Carpet color is yet another consideration. Bring home a large carpet remnant (small samples do not show well) and check the carpet in varying lights from morning to night. Color shifts will occur between sunlight and artificial night lighting, so colors can be deceiving.

When considering carpet price, compare only carpets of the same style and construction. Whatever your choice remember that proper cleaning and care can greatly extend the life of any carpet. The following tips may help you to get all the service your carpet was made to deliver.

Carpet Care and Cleaning

Carpeting is a major decorating investment, so follow good procedures for caring for and cleaning your carpet. Neglect can ruin even a quality carpet, while consideration and routine cleaning can extend the life of even an inexpensive product. Here are tips to help you extend the life of your carpet.

- Buy the best quality product you can afford, one with stain protection built into the product.
- Pad quality is as important as carpet quality in the final job. Beware of dealers who sell you a good pad and install a cheaper product.
- Use commercial-type floor mats at entry doors, and remove your street shoes when you come inside to keep dirt outside.
- Natural skin oils will stain a carpet and make it hold dirt, so don't walk barefoot on carpet.
- Ban food and drink from carpeted areas. If spills occur, clean them up immediately.
- Install a high-capacity central vac or buy a quality upright vacuum cleaner, one with beater bars to beat the dust from the carpet fibers. It is the grit your cheap vacuum can't lift out that will cut the carpet fibers.
- Vacuum often. Carpets that get high traffic should be vacuumed daily.
- Close draperies to shade carpet from direct sunlight that can cause premature fading.

To repair small areas of carpet, buy a carpet repair kit from a professional floor covering tool store. Use the round "cookie cutter" to cut out the damaged carpet area and to cut a patch from a piece of scrap carpet. Peel the backing off an adhesive disc and place it in the hole in the carpet face up; then press the carpet patch in the hole and press firmly in place. Photo by the author.

- Hold a steam iron about 2 inches above the carpet and steam out any dents from furniture legs, etc. Don't place a hot iron directly on nylon or other plastic fibers!
- Have carpets professionally cleaned. Small rental carpet-cleaning units leave detergent and dirt residue in the carpet fibers, causing the carpets to soil quickly after cleaning.
- Have a protective barrier such as Scotchgard sprayed on the carpet each time it is cleaned. The built-in protective barrier in your carpet will break down with use and cleaning, and you should renew carpet protection to keep carpet clean.
- Save any manufacturer's care or warranty information.
- Save a good-sized carpet remnant for future repairs.
- The best all-purpose spot cleaner for carpet that we've found is a product called TECH. You can find TECH at many carpet stores and home centers or contact: TECH Enterprises, 901 Stewart St., Madison, WI 53713.

RADIANT FLOOR HEATING

Rather than close our Floor Covering chapter with the subject of radiant floor heating, perhaps we should have begun the chapter with a discussion of this important subject, because radiant in-floor heating is probably the best and most economical heating system available in the world. Who says so? For one, the Gyp-Crete Corporation, which developed the INFLOOR Heating Systems for both residential and commercial applications. You think a company that sells radiant heating might be biased? Then consider the testimony of a recognized building expert, referring to in-floor or gravity heat: "There is no other 'ideal heat.' Not even the heat of the sun." High praise for the floor heating system from none other than world-famous architect Frank Lloyd Wright.

Frank Lloyd Wright discovered in-floor heating in 1914, while building the Imperial Hotel in Tokyo,

Japan. The bathrooms of the hotel have in-floor heating as a result of a chance visit by Wright to the home of Baron Okura, one of Wright's patrons. After a chilly dinner at the Baron's home, the company was invited into the "Korean room," a room that had in-floor heating, the only warm room in an otherwise cold house. Says Wright: "The climate seemed to have changed. No, it wasn't the coffee: It was spring . . . . The indescribable comfort from being warmed from below was a discovery." (Wright, Frank Lloyd, *The Natural House*, p. 89.)

INFLOOR Heating Systems can use electrical heating cables or polybutylene or cross-linked polyethylene plastic tubes for heat distribution. The electrical heating cables produce resistance heating, while hot water is used to supply heat to floors that have one of the plastic tubing systems. Whatever the heat source, the cable or tubing is embedded in concrete or Gyp-Crete's Therma-Floor Easy-Mix.

The floors can be installed as concrete slab-on-grade or can be poured over wood subfloors in new or remodeling projects. There is even a do-it-yourself INFLOOR kit available to homeowners. First, low-wattage heating cables are attached to the subfloor and connected to a wall-mounted thermostat. A heat sensor is fastened to the subfloor for easy adjustment of floor warmth. Then the cables are embedded in a mortar bed or with Therma-Floor Easy-Mix. The mortar or mix is leveled and smoothed and allowed to harden. Any type of floor covering can be installed atop the concrete floor: wood, tile, vinyl, or carpeting all can be used.

Radiant floors (Wright preferred using the term "gravity" heating) offer uniform temperatures from ceiling to floor (or head to toe), no drafts, and fuel economy. INFLOOR Heating Systems estimates that heat loss is cut by 25 percent, with corresponding reductions in fuel costs. Because the system so readily lends itself to remodeling — no tearing out walls to install heating ducts — the system is worth a look to any remodeling homeowner. The system would be ideal, for example, for installation atop an existing basement concrete floor.

New carpet cleaning kit can be used with a wet/dry vac for immediate cleanup of spills. The cleaning kit uses water from a faucet mixed with cleaning solution to send a spray through the wand onto the carpet. About $50 from Sears. Photo courtesy of Sears.

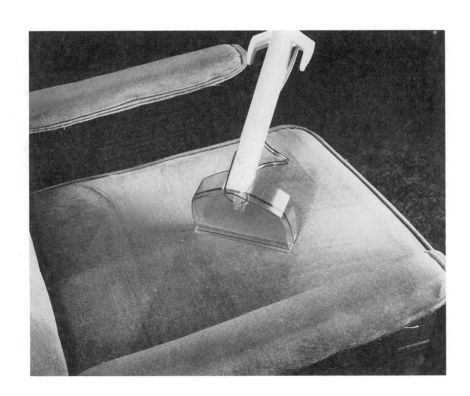

This page and opposite. Light-weight concrete floor product can be poured over hot water tubing or electric heating cables to form radiant heating. Do-it-yourself kit lets a homeowner install radiant heating in bathroom or other floor for about $250. Photos courtesy of INFLOOR Heating Systems.

For more information on the INFLOOR Heating
System contact:

Marketing Services Department
Gyp-Crete Corp.
920 Hamel Road
Hamel, MN 55340
(612) 478-6072

14
Ceiling Options

If your ceilings look like a roller-coaster, or the plaster or ceiling paint is badly cracked or alligatored, and the plaster looks so fragile that your dining room is a designated hard hat area, it may be time to consider options for ceiling removal and replacement. Aside from being an expensive project, complete removal and replacement of ceiling plaster disturbs ceiling insulation, presents a major disposal problem, and is *very dirty*. The good news is that there are a number of possible options to removing the old plaster ceilings, and one of those options should be right for you.

Options to ceiling removal include: applying a skim coat of wallboard compound over the entire ceiling to level, smooth, and conceal minor defects; applying a coverup material such as canvas or fiberglass wall covering over the ceiling; installing a new layer of wallboard over the plaster; furring the ceiling and applying wallboard; installing a new ceiling, including new joists and wallboard, to lower and cover the existing ceiling; and installing a suspended ceiling of gridwork and acoustic or decorative tiles or planks. If you are handy, almost any of these options can be do-it-yourself projects. We will review each option briefly with a discussion of the procedures of each.

WALL COVERING

This is one coverup you should leave to a professional. If you have a plaster ceiling that is reasonably flat and the plaster is tight to the lath, but you have a network of hairline cracks, you can apply

plain canvas (sometimes called "blank stock" because it has no color or pattern) or fiberglass textured wall covering over the ceiling. This will cover the minor cracks and make a smooth surface for decoration. Apply any decoration you choose over the canvas: either wall covering or paint can be used as a finish coat. Fiberglass coverings offer a variety of texture patterns and are usually painted with the product and color of choice.

WALLBOARD

If the ceiling is flat, with no loose plaster or bulges, you can simply install a single layer of 3/8-inch thick wallboard over the existing plaster. Use an electronic stud finder to locate the ceiling joists, and install the wallboard perpendicular to the joists. Use wallboard screws up to 2 inches long to penetrate through the wallboard, plaster, and lath and at least 1/2 inch into the framing joists. Install and finish the wallboard using the directions from Chapter 2 and Chapter 3.

FURRING AND WALLBOARD

If there are loose or bulging sections in the plaster, or the ceiling is very bumpy and uneven, you can first nail up 1 x 2 furring strips and use wooden shims to level the strips. Then you can screw-attach the new wallboard to the furring strips. If you want to upgrade ceiling insulation or improve the soundproofing, install 3/4-inch thick foam insulation board (Styrofoam) between the furring strips.

Ceilings that are badly cracked but still level can be covered with a single layer of wallboard. Use panel adhesives and wallboard screws to apply this new "skin" over old plaster. Photo courtesy of USG.

The first step for furring out a ceiling is to use an electronic stud finder to locate the ceiling joists. Use a pencil to mark each joist location on the wall, about 2 inches below the ceiling so the furring strips will not cover up the pencil marks.

Buy 1 x 2 furring strips that are long enough to span the entire length of the room, or at least 12 feet long. Remember that the furring strips should be installed perpendicular to the existing ceiling joists. Use 8d nails to nail the furring strips in place, 16 inches on center. Do not nail the furring strips tight: leave the strips loose so that you can place wood shims under the strips as required to level the ceiling. Use a straightedge, such as a straight 2 x 4, 8 feet long, to check along the furring strips and make sure the shims make the furring strips level. When you have placed the shims and leveled the furring strips, finish nailing off the strips.

The wallboard thickness to use depends on what you are trying to accomplish. If a flat, new decorat-

ing surface is your only goal, you can install ½-inch thick wallboard panels over the furring strips. However, you can increase the soundproofing and fireproofing qualities of the ceiling by installing ⅝-inch thick wallboard. When you have installed and finished the wallboard (again, see Chapters 2 and Chapter 3) apply the finish of your choice.

LOWERING THE CEILING

Prior to World War II, residential ceiling heights of 9 feet, 10 feet, or more were not uncommon. For most houses, the 8-foot ceiling height became an industry standard during the building boom following World War II. If your plaster ceilings are not only cracked but are higher than today's 8-foot standard height, you can kill two birds with one stone by lowering the ceiling.

To lower a ceiling, first choose a ceiling height and mark the new height on the walls. Use a chalkline to snap a mark at the new height. Be sure to check these marks for level, to ensure that the new ceiling will be level.

When you have marked the ceiling height on the walls, nail a new 1 x 6 ledger at that height, on both long walls of the room. Drive two 8d nails through the ledger board into each wall stud (use the electronic stud finder to find wall studs). Then measure out and mark 16 inch centers on the 1 x 6 ledgers, so the new joists will be 16 inches from the center of one joist to the center of the next joist. Nail metal joist hangers at each of these new joist locations. On the short walls perpendicular to the ledger walls, nail 2 x 2s so you will have nailers to support the edges of the wallboard on all walls.

To ensure a flat ceiling, you should buy the straightest 2 x 6s you can find for use as ceiling joists. Buy the 2 x 6s at a home center so that you can hand-pick the joists for straightness. As you install the joists, hold them on edge and sight along the top edge of the joist. If the joist has a slight bow or curve, install the joist crown side up to make the flattest ceiling. Now cut each joist for length and drop each ceiling joist

Determine ceiling height and make a level chalkline around all the walls. Nail support moldings on all walls at chalkline mark. Photo courtesy of Armstrong.

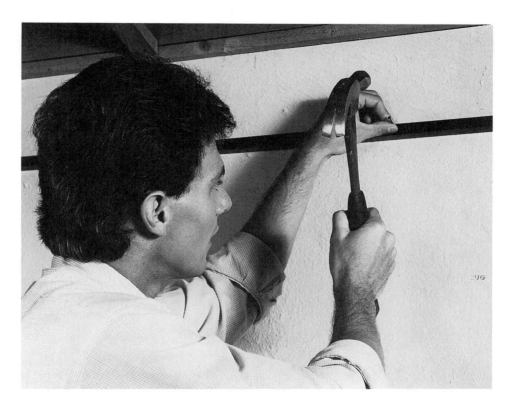

Nail or screw support wires to ceiling or joists above. Level the main metal runners and tie them in place using the wires. This will prevent main runners from sagging when acoustic panels are installed. Photo courtesy of Armstrong.

Snap the cross tees in place on the main runners. When the gridwork of the suspended ceiling is completed, check with a carpenter's level before installing acoustic panels. Photo courtesy of Armstrong.

Install the acoustic ceiling panels by laying them carefully in the gridwork. Wash hands and dust them with talcum powder to avoid soiling the panels during handling. Panels can be removed for replacement or for access to concealed plumbing or wiring. Photo courtesy of Armstrong.

into a pair of metal joist hangers. Drive nails through the nail holes in the joist hangers to hold the joists in place in the hangers. Use a level at each joist to check for level from side to side.

When the joists are in place and level, you can install fiberglass batt insulation between the joists for added thermal value and/or soundproofing. Again, you can install thicker ⅝-inch wallboard for added soundproofing and fireproofing. Finish and paint the wallboard as desired.

SUSPENDED CEILINGS

The options above — new wallboard, furring and wallboard, lowered ceilings — will cover over deteriorating plaster so that it cannot become a falling hazard to home occupants. While they cover and conceal old ceilings from sight, suspended acoustical grid ceilings may be damaged or destroyed by large chunks of falling plaster. It is important that you be sure old plaster will not fail and fall if you install a suspended grid ceiling below it. To avoid any problems, you must remove any loose plaster before starting to install a suspended ceiling.

Suspended grid ceilings can be used anywhere — to conceal an existing ceiling or to finish off an unfinished ceiling. Suspended ceilings of fiberglass panels are often installed in kitchens. The ceiling height can be dropped to match the top of kitchen cabinets, for example, and you can install concealed fluorescent lighting fixtures between the existing ceiling and the suspended ceiling.

Suspended ceilings are also useful for covering ceilings with obstacles, such as basement ceilings. Often plumbing pipes, ductwork, and other obstructions can interfere with ceiling installation. You can drop a suspended ceiling to the lowest point that is obstacle-free and cover up all the obstacles rather than try to frame around them. The panels in suspended ceilings can also be removed so that you can have access to plumbing shut-off valves or for adjusting duct dampers.

To install a suspended ceiling first establish the level of the new ceiling and use a level and chalkline to mark the ceiling height on all walls. Then nail the support moldings to the wall studs at the established lines around the entire perimeter of the room. Next, nail hanger wires to the ceiling studs at the intervals suggested by the ceiling manufacturer. The hanger wires will be used to support and level the main runners of the metal grid. Install the main runners and wrap the support wires around the runners, checking to be sure that the main runners are level as you proceed. Snap the cross tees into place to complete the ceiling grid. Finally, wash and dry your hands, then dust them with talcum powder so you will not get any skin oil on the panels while cutting and handling them. Finally, lay the ceiling panels into place in the grid, cutting any border panels to fit.

CEILING PROBLEMS

Because the ceilings are the largest unbroken surfaces in the house, paint problems such as paint roller or lap marks become more obvious. And because they often support the weight of heavy insulation, ceilings can sag and become wavy. Because ceilings lie underneath the roof where water penetration can damage them, ceilings are subject to problems that are not common to wall or floor surfaces. Following is a list of common ceiling problems and possible solutions to those problems.

Paint roller/lap marks — Because most ceilings are spray textured with a soft spray material, the ceiling surfaces are not sealed, and the texture surfaces are highly absorbent. If you roll latex paint directly over unprimed texture ceilings, the unequal absorption will cause the roller to leave edge or lap marks. Before painting textured ceilings with a flat latex ceiling paint, apply a coat of alkyd (oil) sealer. Once sealed, the finish paint can be applied in an even coating over the ceiling, and you will have no lap or roller marks.

Furring strips, nailed at 12-inch centers over existing ceiling, can support acoustic ceiling tile. The ceiling tile not only offers a clean new ceiling surface but can reduce sound transfer upwards through the ceiling. Photo courtesy of USG.

Check rooftop penetrations such as ventilators and plumbing stacks, common sources of roof leaks. Turbine vents as shown have small bearings that should be lubricated for smooth operation. Photos by the author.

Dirt-streaked ceilings — The wood ceiling joists have less insulating value than ceiling insulation has, and sometimes ceiling insulation is not closely fit against the joists. The result is that the colder part of the ceiling, where the joists are, will attract dust that will cling on the cold spots, and the ceiling will "dirty down" unevenly, with dirt streaks over the ceiling joists. Upgrade your ceiling insulation, with particular attention to covering the joists, and your new paint coat will gray down and age evenly, without having the dirty streaks.

Water stains at corners — Often, ceiling insulation stops just short of the top plate of the exterior walls, leaving an insulation void at the very point or apex of the corner. When interior moisture meets the cold uninsulated corner in cold weather, frost will form at the corner, and the frost will leave yellow water stains when the water dries in warm weather. Have an insulation contractor extend the ceiling insulation so it goes a couple of inches past the top plate of exterior walls, to eliminate the cold spots and the water stains.

Sagging wallboard ceilings — In the early days of wallboard construction, many houses had only 3/8-inch thick wallboard ceilings, and the weight of even a small amount of ceiling insulation would cause the thin wallboard to sag between joists. Even the thicker 1/2-inch wallboard sometimes sagged, and the conditions became worse when we were all told to upgrade our ceiling insulation for energy conservation. Many wallboard ceilings simply are not stiff enough to support the added insulation. The result is sagging wallboard and a wavy or washboard appearance on the ceilings.

If you are building new or remodeling, use only 5/8-inch thick wallboard on ceilings, especially if framing or trusses is set 24 inches on center and the wallboard must support ceiling insulation. If sagging is slight, consult a wallboard contractor, who may be able to install a layer of 5/8-inch wallboard directly over the old wallboard. If sagging is pronounced, you must nail 1 x 2 or thicker furring strips over the old ceiling, shim the furring strips flat with wood shims, and then apply new 5/8-inch wallboard over the furring strips.

Roof leaks — Leaking roofs or plumbing can result in wet wallboard ceilings, and if water is allowed to stand on wallboard, it can cause total deterioration of the wallboard so that replacement is required. The key is to avoid having standing water on the wallboard. When there is water on the backside of wallboard, it will quickly migrate to the nearest joint, and will soak through the wallboard tape and compound, making a wet spot. If you see any sign of wetness on the ceiling, try to investigate from the attic side to see how much water is present at the wet spot. If the ceiling is simply wet, with no standing water, remove the insulation from the wet area so the air can reach and dry the wallboard. If there is standing water, try to block the leak and stop water flow. Then drill or punch a hole in the wallboard at the wet spot so any water can run out. Place a pail or catch basin under the leak to catch the water. Often, if you act quickly, you can avoid extensive water damage if you let the water out. After you find and cure the leak, the only necessary ceiling repair will be to patch the small drain hole you made in the ceiling.

Glossary

ACOUSTICAL MATERIAL — Any building material that has the ability to reduce sound transmission or reflection. Insulation, tiles, and texture spray materials are examples.

AIR SPACE — The cavity formed between building materials in a wall or ceiling; for example, the space between a pair of studs or rafters that is enclosed by wallboard on one side and sheathing material on the opposite side.

ALKYD — A durable synthetic resin used in paint.

BACKING — Wood or other material installed to provide support for finish materials; i.e., scrap wood installed at corners to provide nailers for wallboard.

BASE SHOE — Molding used to cover the crack between the base trim and floor or carpet.

BASEBOARD — Decorative trim used around the perimeter of interior walls, where the floor covering meets the wall.

BEAM CEILING — A ceiling in which the beams are exposed; they may actually support the roof load but often are added for decorative effect only.

BEARING WALL OR PARTITION — Any wall or partition that supports, or bears, weight from above. As opposed to a non-bearing wall or curtain wall, which is a visual barrier supporting no weight but its own.

BLEEDING — Discoloration or stain that comes through paint, such as is caused by smoke or water.

BLIND NAILING — Nails driven so nailheads are not visible. Nails driven at an angle through the tongue of hardwood flooring, so the groove of the adjoining board conceals the nailheads, are "blind nailed."

BOTTOM OR SOLE PLATE — The bottom or framing member of a wall, usually either 2 x 4 or 2 x 6. The plate is nailed to the bottom of the studs and to the floor joist or sheathing below it.

BRIDGING — Wood or steel braces installed in an "X" pattern or diagonally between floor joists to prevent joists from twisting and to transfer loading between joists.

CARPET PAD — A support, often foam, between carpet and subfloor or underlayment.

CAULKING — A compound used to fill cracks.

CEILING JOIST — Structural member providing support for a second story floor and a nailing surface for a lower story ceiling.

CERAMIC TILES — Tiles made of vitreous clay, used as a surface cover or finish on walls, floors, or ceilings.

CHAIR RAIL — A wooden piece of finished trim (usually decorative) placed horizontally at a point along a wall where chairs would be likely to come in contact with it.

CHALK LINE — Metal or plastic container that is teardrop-shaped and holds powdered chalk and a strong cord or line. When the line is pulled out, it is coated with chalk powder: Held by both ends and snapped over a mark, it leaves a line that can be used as a visual or cutting guide.

COMMERCIAL GRADE CARPET — A closely woven, very durable carpet, made to stand up to abuse and heavy traffic.

CORNER BEAD — Sheet metal strip formed to 90 degrees, nailed on outside corners to provide a strong, straight edge for finishing corners in wallboard construction.

CORNER STUDS — Wall studs nailed together to form a 90-degree inside corner, such as where two walls meet.

CROWN MOLDING — Decorative wood trim at the top of an interior wall, where it meets the ceiling.

CURING — A chemical reaction between water and plaster, sometimes called hardening.

CURTAIN WALL — Any wall that does not support weight except its own; a non-bearing wall.

CUTTING IN — When using a paint roller, to paint a strip with a brush. Painting a small area along the wall/ceiling line to allow complete coverage of areas the roller cannot reach.

DEAD LOAD — The weight of all the materials in a building, added together, is called the dead load. The live load is the weight of the occupants and furnishings.

DEADENING — Materials or building techniques intended to stop noise transfer.

DRYWALL — Panels consisting of a plaster core and front and back covers of paper, used for interior finish in place of plaster. Also called plaster board, wallboard, or Sheetrock, which is a trade name.

DRYWALL MUD — Joint compound; the material used to hide seams and screw heads in finished wallboard.

ENAMEL — Paint, usually oil-base, used in high soil areas such as trim and doors.

FALSE CEILING — A drop or suspended ceiling, hung on metal or wood grids, to permit covering exposed ducts, pipes, or beams.

FEATHER — To trowel to a thin edge, as when finishing wallboard joints.

FLAT PAINT — Interior paint containing a high proportion of pigment and drying to a flat or lusterless finish.

FLOAT — To spread joint compound smooth.

FLOOR JOIST — A structural member used to support the floor of a house.

FRAMING — The portion of the building that forms the support; studs, joists, and rafters are framing.

FURRING CHANNEL — The horizontal support in the grid that holds a suspended ceiling.

GLOSS PAINT — Paint containing a relatively low proportion of pigment and drying to a sheen.

GROUT — Material used to fill spaces or cracks between tile during installation.

GYPSUM — Optional term referring to wallboard; more specifically, the plaster core between the two layers of paper on a wallboard panel.

INSULATION — Any material that provides a barrier to passage of heat, electricity, or sound.

JOINT COMPOUND — The substance used to hide seams and screw heads in finished wallboard. Also called drywall mud.

JOIST — A framing member, spaced 16 inches or 24 inches on center, that supports either the floor or the ceiling.

JOIST HANGER — A metal device, shaped like a "U", used to connect two joists or a joist and beam at right angles to each other.

LATEX — Water-base paint.

LATH — Base material for plaster; can be wood, gypsum, or steel (wire).

LIVE LOAD — Weight of materials that are not part of the house, such as furniture and appliances; also weight (combined) of occupants of house. As opposed to "dead load," the weight of the house itself.

MESH — Metal wire reinforcing base for plaster.

MOISTURE BARRIER — Any material (usually building paper or polyethylene plastic sheets) used to block the flow of moisture or vapor through walls, ceilings, or floors.

NAIL POPS — Caused by shrinkage of framing members after wallboard is installed. Also called fastener failure, and is also common in screw application of wallboard. Prevention: Use construction adhesives, dry lumber.

NONBEARING WALL — Wall or partition that provides a curtain or barrier to passage but does not support any structural load.

ON CENTER — The interval between framing members, such as studs, joists, or rafters, is always expressed as "on center," or "o.c.", rather than "between" to avoid confusion. The measurement refers to the distance from the center of one framing member to the center of the next framing member.

PARQUET — Small squares of wood applied to a floor in a pattern.

PARTICLE BOARD — A composite of wood chips bonded and pressed together to form a sheet used for subflooring or sheathing.

PLASTER BOARD — Term used to refer to drywall, wallboard, gypsum board.

PRIMER — First coat of paint used to prepare surface for finish coat.

R VALUE — The "R" stands for "resistance" to heat flow, and is a means of measuring the value of materials used for thermal insulation.

SEMI-GLOSS — Paint or enamel that dries to a luster but is not glossy or shiny.

SOUND TRANSMISSION — The sound that passes through a given material or building unit; usually expressed in decibels as the unit of measurement.

SPACKLE — A pasty material used to fill small cracks and holes.

SPAN — The distance separating supporting members such as beams or bearing walls.

STC — Sound Transmission Class; relates via decibel loss how resistant a building unit is to sound passage.

STIPPLE — Rough or textured coating applied to ceilings.

STUD — The framing members that support the walls, to which wallboard is fastened on the inside and sheathing/siding on the outside.

SUBFLOOR — The first or primary layer of wood that covers the top of the floor joists.

SUSPENDED CEILING — A ceiling usually supported by wires and hung beneath the level of the joists. Suspended ceilings are often chosen where ducts, pipes, or framing prevent installation of a level ceiling.

TAPING — Term used in wallboard construction that refers to the entire process of finishing the wallboard, including sealing the joints with wallboard tape and applying two trowel coats that level the joints.

UNDERLAYMENT — Material used as a base for applying some finish material, such as carpet underlayment.

WALLBOARD — Panels consisting of a plaster core and front and back covers of paper, used for interior finish in place of plaster. Also called drywall, plaster board, or Sheetrock, which is a trade name.

Appendix

Checklist — Drywall

NOTES

❏ Before application begins, check that all wiring, plumbing, and framing are in place. Make final check of insulation and vapor barrier.

❏ Use the best installation techniques: all wallboard applied perpendicular to framing; 1-inch wallboard screws as fasteners; wallboard adhesive used in all areas with no vapor barrier.

❏ Be sure no vapor barrier is added in bath areas where water-resistant wallboard is used. Vapor barrier under water-resistant board is prohibited by manufacturers.

❏ Water-resistant board will sag if used on ceilings. Use regular wallboard for bath ceilings.

❏ All-metal, nail-on corner beads to be used on all outside corners. Glue-on corner bead can be easily damaged by impact blows.

❏ All outside corner bead, joints, nail or screw heads to receive not less than three coats of taping/finishing compound. Texture paint will not flatten or "hide" joints with excessive shrinkage or two-coat finish.

❏ Spray texture ceilings will look better if they receive a first coat of primer. Prime coat ceilings before spraying.

❏ To spray texture new wallboard ceilings, overspray at the corners, then scrape away the texture on the walls. Check to be sure the scraping process has left the corners smooth, without piles of texture at corners to interfere with wall decoration.

❏ At night, with lights out, apply strong sidelight to walls, using trouble light with bare bulb held near wall. Look down the wall and check for hollow nail or screw heads, hollow or "starved" joints, loose or bubbled tape, rough edges. This inspection is most easily done after walls are primed.

❏ Mark any blemishes or rough spots with a pencil, so you can find them in daylight. Do not use a ballpoint pen or marker — the ink bleeds through most paints.

❏ Check inside corners to be sure they are square, not loaded with taping compound. Corners that are not square make trim application difficult.

Checklist — Wall Covering

NOTES

❏ Choose a room with no unusual corners or features for your first try at hanging wall covering. Avoid wall coverings that have stripes or geometric patterns that will be hard to match.

❏ Buy wall coverings that are vinyl and prepasted. Buy strippable coverings for easy future removal.

❏ Buy a Bubblestick that serves as both level and straightedge for cutting coverings.

❏ Wall covering tools may be rented or borrowed from the wall covering dealer. Using a wall covering table makes work faster, easier.

❏ Use a razor knife with break-off tips, and use a fresh tip for each cut. Dull razor knives will tear or rip wall covering.

❏ Use a wall size to prevent adhesives from soaking into the wall, and to maximize "open" time or work time before adhesive dries.

❏ Observe soak time recommended on wall covering. As you pull wall covering from the soak tray, check to be sure all adhesive on covering has liquified.

❏ Fill a plastic pail with warm water. Use a sponge to wipe down wall covering and to remove adhesive from the finish side of the covering. Change water and rinse sponge frequently.

❏ Turn off electricity to the room you are working in. Wet wall covering can conduct electricity and generate a dangerous shock to the worker. Be especially careful when hanging metallic coverings.

❏ Turn off room thermostat and keep windows closed to avoid drafts that will dry the covering adhesive too quickly. If necessary, in dry weather, place a humidifier in the room to keep humidity levels high and extend work time.

❏ Check wall coverings for pattern match, closed seams, and uniformity of color and pattern.

❏ When removing old wall covering, first peel up a corner and try to pull the covering off. If the covering is strippable, pull the covering off and wash the walls to remove adhesive and paper residue.

Checklist — Wall Covering cont'd

❑ If wall covering does not peel off, use a serrated tool to abrade the surface so water can enter and dissolve the adhesive.

❑ Add a remover such as Savogran's FAST Wallpaper Remover to a pail of hot water. The remover will speed up softening of the adhesive.

❑ Apply the hot water/remover solution to the covering, using a sponge or sponge floor mop. Saturate the paper with repeated applications of water before you begin scraping or removal efforts.

❑ Test the covering with a scraper to see if it peels away easily. If it does not, apply more water and wait until water has time to soften adhesive.

❑ When wall covering is removed, wipe down walls with warm water and remover solution, keeping water and sponge clean. This step will remove any adhesive residue.

❑ To avoid having a soggy paper mess, place a trash container in the work area and placed removed paper or covering directly in the container as you remove it from the wall.

❑ Inspect wall covering job lit from an oblique angle. This will reveal any adhesive or other stains on the face or surface of the covering.

❑ Buy and save at least one extra roll of each wall covering pattern for future repairs. This ensures that the material will be available if you need it in the future.

❑ Keep a diary of your job and record the brand and color of the paint, the name and stock number of the wall covering, brand and color of carpeting, etc. Update the book as you redecorate. When you sell the house, this book will be a welcome gift to the new owner.

NOTES

Checklist — Painting

NOTES

❏ Paint costs are small compared to the labor of painting. Avoid discount paints.

❏ Use a liquid sander product when preparing woodwork and trim for painting. This eliminates the work and dust from sanding.

❏ Check walls, ceilings, and woodwork for lead paint before sanding or repainting. Buy a lead test kit (eight swabs) for $13.50. Call 1-800-262-LEAD (Hybrivet Systems, Inc., Framingham, MA 01701).

❏ If lead tests indicate lead contamination, call health department for name of a lead abatement contractor.

❏ Choose latex paints for most interior projects for less pollution, water cleanup.

❏ Alkyd (oil-based) paints are still preferred for painting cabinets, furniture.

❏ To be able to use stairs while repainting them, paint every other step. Allow to dry, then paint the remaining steps.

❏ Coat spray-textured ceilings with an alkyd sealer, allow to dry, then apply a finish coat of flat latex paint.

❏ Prime all new wallboard with USG First Coat or other heavy-bodied latex paint. Finish coat to be a quality latex of prescribed gloss level — flat, semi-gloss, or high gloss.

❏ When paint is dry, check walls for covering, neatness, corners neatly cut in.

❏ Spackle any blemishes overlooked during wallboard taping, or nicks and scratches on walls inflicted during trim and finish steps.

❏ Check all painted surfaces to be sure the paint is evenly applied: no lap marks, roller ridges, or brush marks permitted.

❏ Check trim, paneling, and cabinetry for paint spatters and runs. Clean spatters while paint is soft.

❏ All trim should be painted at least two coats; nail holes to be puttied.

❏ Slip the foot from a pair of pantyhose over your hand and move the covered hand over finished wood trim. There should be no snags or rough spots.

Checklist — Painting cont'd

❏ Check door edges and top and bottom ends to be sure they are sealed so moisture cannot penetrate.

❏ Pay attention to detail. Check inside of cabinet doors, cabinet and closet shelves, being sure nothing has been skipped.

❏ Check hardware, ceramic tile, and countertops for paint spatters and runs. Clean up while the paint is fresh.

❏ Leftover paint can be used for touchups. Unused full gallons may be returned for refund. Order carefully: custom-mixed colors cannot be returned.

❏ Check ladder load limits (on ladder label) before you begin work. Be sure the ladder will support weight of worker, materials, and tools.

❏ Observe safety rules. Wear a dust mask when sanding. Provide adequate ventilation. (Use a fan, if available, to exhaust paint fumes.) Wash hands before eating, drinking, or smoking.

❏ Maintain ventilation until all the material odors have dissipated.

NOTES

_____
_____
_____
_____
_____
_____
_____
_____
_____
_____
_____
_____
_____
_____

Lead Hazards

If your house was built before 1978, it probably was coated with lead paint. Lead was used to improve the durability of both interior and exterior paints. Recent studies have shown, however, that the health risks of lead were underrated. Not only are permissible lead levels lower than was earlier thought, but a growing list of objects and substances found in the home are now suspected of being health risks via their lead content. Among suspect items are paint, dust, dishes, crystal, food cans (because of seams that are lead-soldered), solder (in copper water piping), and even the soil of the yard where your children play (washed there from old lead-based house paint).

Renovating or redecorating your house may expose you and your family to lead poisoning. Young children are especially prone to lead problems, because they play in the dirt and may put lead-contaminated objects in their mouths. Although lead can produce learning and behavior problems and even mental retardation in children, there are no early symptoms. If you suspect lead poisoning or exposure, take your child to a local clinic or pediatrician for a simple blood test.

It is not advisable to try removing lead yourself. Increasingly, states are mandating that all lead removal be done by professionals who are trained in proper procedures.

To obtain simple and inexpensive test swabs for lead, call 1-800-262-LEAD. LeadCheck products are sold by HybriVet Systems, Inc. (Framingham, MA 01701). An eight-pack of swabs costs $13.50; sixteen swabs cost $24.95; each plus $3.50 for shipping and handling. Full test directions for each category of lead are included with the kit.

If you are buying a house that was built before 1978, check the house for lead problems before you move in. The best time for lead removal is while the house is empty. If you test your home and find lead is present, you can get help. Check with your local health department or the Environmental Protection Agency office nearest you to direct you to a licensed contractor who handles lead abatement.

Personal Lead Inspection Report

INTERIOR ROOM	Kitchen	Bathroom	Living Room	Bedroom 1	Bedroom 2	Bedroom 3									
Upper Walls															
Lower Walls															
Chair Rail															
Baseboards															
Door															
Door Casing/Jamb															
Window Sill/Apron															
Window Casing															
Header/Stops															
Sash/Mullions															
Exterior Sill															
Parting Bead															
Closet Walls															
Closet Door															
Door Casing/Jamb															
Baseboards															
Shelves															
Floor															
Ceiling															
Cabinets															
Shelves															
Drawers															

EXTERIOR	North Side	East Side	South Side	West Side
Siding				
Dripboard				
Skirt				
Cornerboards				
Upper Trim				
Lower Trim				
Door				
Casing/Jamb				
Threshold				
Window Sill				
Window Casing				
Sash/Mullions				
Cellar Windows				
Bulkhead				
Fences				
Decks				
Porches				
Garage Door				
Casing/Jamb				

STAIRCASE				
Upper Walls				
Lower Walls				
Chair Rail				
Treads				
Risers				
Railing/Cap				
Handrails				
Balusters				
Newel Posts				
Stringer				
Baseboards				
Window Sill/Apron				
Window Casing				
Header/Stops				
Sash/Mullions				
Exterior Sill				
Parting Bead				
Doors				
Ceiling				

Chart reproduced courtesy of HybriVet Systems, Inc.

Index

FIND THIS BOOK HELPFUL?
CHECK THESE OTHER USER-FRIENDLY TITLES* FROM BETTERWAY ...

The Complete Guide to Contracting Your Home, 2nd Edition — A Step-by-Step Guide for Managing Home Construction, by David L. McGuerty and Kent Lester. 288 pages, illustrations, forms, checklists. 1-55870-229-6. $18.95.

The Complete Guide to Residential Deck Construction—From the Simplest to the Most Sophisticated, by Greg Roy. 176 pages, photos (color and B&W), illustrations, forms. 1-55870-231-8. $16.95.

The Complete Guide to Buying Your First Home— Roadmap to a Successful, Worry-Free Closing, by R. Dodge Woodson. 216 pages, forms, glossary. 1-55870-228-8. $14.95.

Get the Most for Your Remodeling Dollar—How to Save Money, Save Time, and Avoid Frustration, by R. Dodge Woodson. 216 pages, photos, illustrations, checklists. 1-55870-211-3. $16.95.

The Complete Guide to Lumber Yards and Home Centers — A Consumer's Guide to Choosing and Using Building Materials and Tools, by Gary D. Branson. 176 pages, photos, illustrations. 1-55870-209-1. 14.95.

The Complete Guide to Floors, Walls, and Ceilings— A Comprehensive Do-it-Yourself Handbook, by Gary D. Branson. 176 pages, photos, illustrations. 1-55870-230-X. $14.95.

The Complete Guide to Barrier-Free Housing—Convenient Living for the Elderly and Physically Handicapped, by Gary D. Branson. 176 pages, photos, illustrations. 1-55870-188-5. $14.95.

The Complete Guide to Recycling at Home—How to Take Responsibility, Savce Money, and Protect the Environment, by Gary D. Branson. 176 pages, photos, illustrations. 1-55870-189-3. $14.95.

The Complete Guide to Remodeling Your Basement —How to Create New Living Space the Professional Way, by Gary D. Branson. 170 pages, photos, illustrations, checklists. 1-55870-162-1. $14.95.

The Complete Guide to Understanding and Caring for Your Home—A Practical Handbook for Knowledgeable Homeowners, by James Madorma. 272 pages, photos, illustrations. 1-55870-210-5. $18.95.

The Home Buyer's Inspection Guide, by James Madorma. 176 pages, illustrations, forms, checklists. 1-55870-146-X. $11.95.

The Complete Guide to Landscape Design, Renovation, and Maintenance—A Practical Handbook for the Home Landscape Gardener, by Cass Turnbull. 192 pages, illustrations. 1-55870-208-3. $14.95.

The Complete Guide to Decorative Landscaping with Brick and Masonry, by Edward J. Heddy and Pete Peterson. 160 pages, photos, illustrations. 1-55870-145-1. $11.95.

The Complete Guide to Painting Your Home—Doing it the Way a Professional Does, Inside and Out, by Jack Luts and Pete Peterson. 160 pages, photos, illustrations, forms. 1-55870-119-2. $11.95.

The Complete Guide to Home Security — How to Protect Your Family and Home from Harm, by David Alan Wacker. 192 pages, photos, illustrations, checklists. 1-55870-163-X. $14.95.

The Complete Guide to Decorating Your Home — How to Become Your Own Interior Designer, by Rima Kamen. 288 pages, photos (color and B&W), illustrations. 1-55870-117-6. $18.95.

* All in the large, 8½ x 11 format.

Please try your favorite bookseller first. If all else fails, tell us what you want. Send the price of the book plus $2.50 for UPS shipping (for any number of books) to Betterway Publications, Inc., P.O. Box 219, Crozet, VA 22932.